Reading Shakespeare can be a real headache

That's why we've put this book together.

We've put notes handily next to the play so you don't have to go hunting for "Note 136". That means you can understand what all the weird bits mean without losing the flow of the play.

We've written the notes in plain English to make it just that bit easier.

There's even the odd bit of ever-so-nearly entertaining humour in the notes and pictures to help you breeze through the toughest of scenes.

We've done our bit — the rest is up to you.

MACBETH — TRAGIC COMICS

CONTENTS

Published by Coordination Group Publications, Ltd.

Editors:
Taissa Csáky
Tim Major
Becky May
Katherine Reed

ISBN: 1 84146 120 2
Groovy website: www.cgpbooks.co.uk
Jolly bits of clipart from CorelDRAW
Printed by Elanders Hindson, Newcastle upon Tyne.

Text, design, layout and original illustrations © Coordination Group Publications Ltd

ACT 1 SCENE 1
A deserted place

Thunder and lightning. Enter three WITCHES.

FIRST WITCH   When shall we three meet again?
   In thunder, lightning, or in rain?
SECOND WITCH   When the hurly-burly's done,
   When the battle's lost and won.
THIRD WITCH   That will be ere the set of sun.   5
FIRST WITCH   Where the place?
SECOND WITCH   Upon the heath.
THIRD WITCH   There to meet with Macbeth.
FIRST WITCH   I come, Graymalkin!
SECOND WITCH   Paddock calls.
THIRD WITCH   Anon!   10
ALL   Fair is foul, and foul is fair,
   Hover through the fog and filthy air.
                        Exeunt

hurly-burly = *commotion*

4 *A battle between the Scottish King and his army against a rebel army supported by the King of Norway.*

ere = *before*

8-10 *The Witches are talking to their 'familiars' — i.e. creatures like owls and black cats.*

anon = *coming!*

ACT 1 SCENE 2
A camp near Forres

Alarum within. Enter DUNCAN, MALCOLM, DONALBAIN,
   LENNOX, *with Attendants, meeting a bleeding* CAPTAIN.

DUNCAN   What bloody man is that? He can report,
   As seemeth by his plight, of the revolt
   The newest state.
MALCOLM   This is the sergeant
   Who like a good and hardy soldier fought
   'Gainst my captivity. Hail, brave friend!   5
   Say to the king the knowledge of the broil
   As thou didst leave it.
CAPTAIN   Doubtful it stood;
   As two spent swimmers, that do cling together
   And choke their art. The merciless Macdonald —
   Worthy to be a rebel, for to that   10
   The multiplying villanies of nature
   Do swarm upon him — from the western isles
   Of kerns and gallowglasses is supplied;
   And fortune, on his damnèd quarrel smiling,
   Showed like a rebel's whore: but all's too weak: 15
   For brave Macbeth — well he deserves that name —
   Disdaining fortune, with his brandished steel,
   Which smoked with bloody execution,
   Like Valour's minion carved out his passage
   Till he faced the slave;   20
   Which ne'er shook hands, nor bade farewell to him,
   Till he unseamed him from the nave to the chops,
   And fixed his head upon our battlements.
DUNCAN   O valiant cousin! Worthy gentleman!

alarum = *blast of trumpets from the battlefield*

1-3 *'Who's that bloke covered in blood? By the look of him he'll be able to tell us the latest news from the battle.'*

broil = *fight*

7-9 *'You couldn't tell which side would win — they were like two drowning men, clinging together and dragging each other under.'*

9-13 *'Macdonald has hired mercenaries from the western isles. It makes sense that he's a rebel — he's rotten through and through.'*

14-15 *'Luck seemed to be on his side, but it wasn't enough.'*

brandished steel = *sword*

19-20 *Macbeth 'slashed his way through the battle until he reached that scum Macdonald.'*

minion = *favourite*

21-22 *'He didn't hang about. He sliced him from his belly to his jaw.'*

CAPTAIN   As whence the sun 'gins his reflection   25
Shipwrecking storms and direful thunders break,
So from that spring whence comfort seemed to come
Discomfort swells. Mark, King of Scotland, mark:
No sooner justice had with valour armed
Compelled these skipping kerns to trust their heels,   30
But the Norwegian lord surveying vantage,
With furbished arms and new supplies of men,
Began a fresh assault.

DUNCAN   Dismayed not this
Our captains, Macbeth and Banquo?

CAPTAIN   Yes —
As sparrows eagles, or the hare the lion.   35
If I say sooth, I must report they were
As cannons overcharged with double cracks, so they
Doubly redoubled strokes upon the foe:
Except they meant to bathe in reeking wounds,
Or memorise another Golgotha,   40
I cannot tell —
But I am faint, my gashes cry for help.

DUNCAN   So well thy words become thee as thy wounds;
They smack of honour both. Go get him surgeons.

Exit CAPTAIN, *attended.*

Who comes here?

MALCOLM *(Enter ROSSE)* The worthy Thane of Rosse.   45

LENOX   What a haste looks through his eyes! So should he look
That seems to speak things strange.

ROSSE   God save the King!

DUNCAN   Whence camest thou, worthy thane?

ROSSE   From Fife, great King;
Where the Norwegian banners flout the sky
And fan our people cold.   50
Norway himself, with terrible numbers,
Assisted by that most disloyal traitor
The Thane of Cawdor, began a dismal conflict;
Till that Bellona's bridegroom, lapped in proof,
Confronted him with self-comparisons,   55
Point against point rebellious, arm 'gainst arm,
Curbing his lavish spirit. And, to conclude,
The victory fell on us.

DUNCAN   Great happiness!

ROSSE   That now Sweno,
The Norways' king, craves composition.   60
Nor would we deign him burial of his men
Till he disbursed, at Saint Colme's Inch
Ten thousand dollars to our general use.

DUNCAN   No more that Thane of Cawdor shall deceive
Our bosom interest: go pronounce his present death,   65
And with his former title greet Macbeth.

ROSSE   I'll see it done.

DUNCAN   What he hath lost, noble Macbeth hath won.

Exeunt

25-28 'It seemed as if everything was going better, but then it all went wrong again — it was as though a big storm had blown up even though the sun was shining.'
mark = pay attention

29-33 'No sooner had Macbeth's bravery scared off the mercenaries than the King of Norway sent a whole new lot of men and arms for a fresh attack.'
furbished = polished

33-34 'Didn't this worry Macbeth and Banquo?'

34-35 'About as much as sparrows worry eagles and hares scare lions.'
say sooth = tell the truth

37 'like cannons with a double-load of ammunition'

39-41 'I don't know if they wanted to be covered in bleeding wounds, or recreate the Crucifixion...'
become = suit

46-47 'He's got a funny look in his eyes. He looks like he's got some odd news.'

flout = mock

Bellona's bridegroom = Mars, the god of war. Here it means Macbeth.

lapped in proof = wearing armour

55-57 '...fought as well as the King fought, sword against sword, weapon against weapon, cutting him down to size.'

the victory fell on us = we won

composition = peace treaty

61-63 'Nor would we let him bury his men till he had handed over ten thousand dollars at Saint Colme's Inch...'

deceive our bosom interest = act against my interests

present = immediate

ACT 1 SCENE 3
A heath

> Macbeth and Banquo meet the Witches out on the moor. The Witches say Macbeth is going to be Thane of Cawdor and end up as King. They say Banquo's descendants will be kings, too.

Thunder. Enter the three WITCHES.

FIRST WITCH   Where hast thou been, sister?

SECOND WITCH   Killing swine.

THIRD WITCH   Sister, where thou?

FIRST WITCH   A sailor's wife had chestnuts in her lap
And munched, and munched, and munched.
                          'Give me', quoth I.
'Aroint thee, witch!' the rump-fed ronyon cries.   5
Her husband's to Aleppo gone, master o'th'Tiger:
But in a sieve I'll thither sail,
And like a rat without a tail,
I'll do, I'll do, and I'll do.

SECOND WITCH   I'll give thee a wind.   10

FIRST WITCH   Thou'rt kind.

THIRD WITCH   And I another.

FIRST WITCH   I myself have all the other,
And the very ports they blow,
All the quarters that they know   15
I'th'shipman's card.
I'll drain him dry as hay:
Sleep shall neither night nor day
Hang upon his penthouse lid;
He shall live a man forbid.   20
Weary sennights nine times nine,
Shall he dwindle, peak, and pine.
Though his bark cannot be lost,
Yet it shall be tempest-tossed.
Look what I have.   25

SECOND WITCH   Show me, show me.

FIRST WITCH   Here I have a pilot's thumb,
Wrecked as homeward he did come.

Drum within

THIRD WITCH   A drum, a drum!
Macbeth doth come.   30

ALL   The weïrd sisters, hand in hand,
Posters of the sea and land,
Thus do go, about, about,
Thrice to thine, and thrice to mine,
And thrice again, to make up nine.   35
Peace — the charm's wound up.

Enter MACBETH *and* BANQUO.

MACBETH   So foul and fair a day I have not seen.

BANQUO   How far is't called to Forres? What are these,
So withered and so wild in their attire,
That look not like th'inhabitants o'th'earth,   40
And yet are on't? Live you, or are you aught
That man may question? You seem to understand me,
By each at once her choppy finger laying

quoth I = *I said*

5 '"Get lost, witch!" shouted the spoilt cow.'

6 'Her husband's captain of the 'Tiger', and he's gone to Aleppo.'

7-8 People believed witches could turn into animals (ones without tails), and sail in sieves.

10, 12 The other Witches will help make winds blow against the captain's ship.

14-15 'Winds will blow from all ports and from all corners of the compass.'

shipman's card = *compass*

18-24 'The storms will stop the captain sleeping for weeks and weeks, so he'll get all weak. His ship won't sink, but it'll be thrown about in storms.'

penthouse lid = *eyelid*

sennights = *7 nights (a week)*

31-35 This is a little spell they're casting. The numbers 3, 9 (and 7) were supposed to have magic powers.

thrice = *three times*

posters = *people who travel quickly*

36 'Quiet now, the spell's cast.'

38-42 'What are these weird looking things, that don't look like Earth-dwellers, but are on the Earth? Are you alive, or are you something humans can talk to?'

4

44-46 *'You must be women, but as you've got beards, that's hard to believe.'*

Upon her skinny lips; you should be women,
And yet your beards forbid me to interpret   45
That you are so.

47-49 This bit's dead important — the Witches call Macbeth Thane of Glamis (which he knows he is), then Thane of Cawdor (which he is but he doesn't know it yet), and then say he'll be King.

MACBETH   Speak if you can: what are you?

FIRST WITCH   All hail Macbeth! Hail to thee, Thane of Glamis.

SECOND WITCH   All hail Macbeth! Hail to thee, Thane of Cawdor.

THIRD WITCH   All hail Macbeth that shalt be King hereafter!

Glamis is pronounced strangely: it's Glarms, not Gla-miss.

BANQUO   Good sir, why do you start, and seem to fear   50
Things that do sound so fair? I'th'name of truth

52 'Are you imaginary or real?'

Are ye fantastical, or that indeed
Which outwardly ye show? My noble partner

54-55 'saying Macbeth is Thane of Cawdor and will be King'

You greet with present grace and great prediction
Of noble having and of royal hope   55
That he seems rapt withal. To me you speak not.

rapt withal = completely spellbound

If you can look into the seeds of time
And say which grain will grow and which will not,

59-60 Banquo wants to know about his own future.

Speak then to me, who neither beg nor fear
Your favours nor your hate.   60

FIRST WITCH   Hail!

SECOND WITCH   Hail!

THIRD WITCH   Hail!

64-66 Banquo is less than Macbeth because he won't be King. But he's also more, because his sons will be kings, and he's a better man too.

FIRST WITCH   Lesser than Macbeth, and greater.

SECOND WITCH   Not so happy, yet much happier.   65

THIRD WITCH   Thou shalt get kings, though thou be none.
So all hail Macbeth and Banquo!

FIRST WITCH   Banquo and Macbeth, all hail!

MACBETH   Stay, you imperfect speakers. Tell me more.

70-74 Macbeth inherited the title Thane of Glamis from his dad, Sinel. He doesn't see how he can be Thane of Cawdor, though, and thinks being King is unlikely.

By Sinel's death, I know I am Thane of Glamis,   70
But how of Cawdor? The Thane of Cawdor lives
A prosperous gentleman, and to be king
Stands not within the prospect of belief,
No more than to be Cawdor. Say from whence

74-75 'Tell me where you got this info from.'

You owe this strange intelligence, or why   75
Upon this blasted heath you stop our way
With such prophetic greeting? Speak, I charge you.

                    WITCHES *vanish.*

whither = where

BANQUO   The earth hath bubbles, as the water has,
And these are of them. Whither are they vanished?

corporal = of flesh and blood

MACBETH   Into the air, and what seemed corporal,   80
Melted, as breath into the wind. Would they had stayed.

would = I wish

BANQUO   Were such things here as we do speak about?

82-84 'Were they really here, or have we lost our marbles?'

Or have we eaten on the insane root,
That takes the reason prisoner?

MACBETH   Your children shall be kings.

BANQUO   You shall be King.   85

MACBETH   And Thane of Cawdor too: went it not so?

BANQUO   To th'self same tune and words — who's here?

                    Enter ROSSE *and* ANGUS

Rosse and Angus come to tell Macbeth that he's the new Thane of Cawdor. Macbeth starts wondering if what the Witches said will come true after all.

Act 1, Scene 3

ROSSE   The King hath happily received, Macbeth,
        The news of thy success, and when he reads
        Thy personal venture in the rebels' sight,   90
        His wonders and his praises do contend
        Which should be thine or his. Silenced with that,
        In viewing o'er the rest o'th'selfsame day,
        He finds thee in the stout Norwegian ranks,
        Nothing afeard of what thyself didst make,   95
        Strange images of death. As thick as tale
        Came post with post, and every one did bear
        Thy praises in his kingdom's great defence,
        And poured them down before him.
ANGUS   We are sent
        To give thee from our royal master thanks;   100
        Only to herald thee into his sight,
        Not pay thee.
ROSSE   And for an earnest of a greater honour,
        He bade me, from him, call thee Thane of Cawdor:
        In which addition, hail most worthy Thane,   105
        For it is thine.
BANQUO   What, can the devil speak true?
MACBETH   The Thane of Cawdor lives. Why do you dress me
        In borrowed robes?
ANGUS   Who was the Thane, lives yet,
        But under heavy judgement bears that life
        Which he deserves to lose.   110
        Whether he was combined with those of Norway,
        Or did line the rebel with hidden help
        And vantage, or that with both he laboured
        In his country's wrack, I know not,
        But treasons capital, confessed and proved,   115
        Have overthrown him.
MACBETH (Aside)   Glamis, and Thane of Cawdor:
        The greatest is behind. — Thanks for your pains. —
        (To Banquo) Do you not hope your children shall be kings,
        When those that gave the Thane of Cawdor to me
        Promised no less to them?
BANQUO   That, trusted home,   120
        Might yet enkindle you unto the crown,
        Besides the Thane of Cawdor. But 'tis strange,
        And oftentimes, to win us to our harm,
        The instruments of darkness tell us truths,
        Win us with honest trifles — to betray's   125
        In deepest consequence.
        Cousins, a word, I pray you.
MACBETH (Aside)   Two truths are told,
        As happy prologues to the swelling act
        Of the imperial theme. — I thank you, gentlemen. —
        This supernatural soliciting   130
        Cannot be ill, cannot be good. If ill,
        Why hath it given me earnest of success,
        Commencing in a truth? I am Thane of Cawdor.

88-92 'The King's heard about how bravely you fought in the battle. When he hears the detail he'll be even more impressed, and hardly know what to give you as a reward.'

post with post = message after message

101 'to be your official escort to the King'

106 Banquo realises the Witches' first prediction has come true.

107-108 'How can I be Thane of Cawdor when the old one's still alive?'

108-116 'The old Thane of Cawdor is going to be killed soon. I don't know the details of what he did, but he's confessed and it's been proved he was a traitor.'

wrack = ruin

117 'The greatest is yet to come.'

120-127 'If you believe what they said, you're going to be King as well as Thane of Cawdor. On the other hand, evil creatures sometimes get people to trust them by saying a few things that are true — then get them into big trouble.'

127-129 'The two true things the Witches said are just the build-up to the important bit about being King.'

130-140 'The predictions can't be good, and they can't be bad. If they're bad, why has part of it come true? But if they're good, why do I keep thinking of killing Duncan, which really scares me? Nothing is as frightening as my own imagination. My thoughts are taking me over and stopping me doing anything'

If good, why do I yield to that suggestion,
Whose horrid image doth unfix my hair   135
And make my seated heart knock at my ribs
Against the use of nature? Present fears
Are less than horrible imaginings.
My thought, whose murder yet is but fantastical,
Shakes so my single state of man that function   140
Is smothered in surmise, and nothing is,
But what is not.

BANQUO   Look how our partner's rapt.

rapt = deep in thought

143-144 'If my fate is to be King, fate may make me King, even if I do nothing.'

MACBETH   If chance will have me King, why, chance may crown me,
Without my stir.

144-146 'Macbeth's stunned by the good news.'

BANQUO   New honours come upon him
Like our strange garments, cleave not to their mould,   145
But with the aid of use.

146-147 'Whatever happens will happen.'

MACBETH   Come what come may,
Time and the hour runs through the roughest day.

BANQUO   Worthy Macbeth, we stay upon your leisure.

MACBETH   Give me your favour. My dull brain was wrought

149-152 'Sorry, I was miles away. I'll remember what you've done for me. Let's go and see the King.'

With things forgotten. Kind gentlemen, your pains   150
Are registered where every day I turn
The leaf to read them. Let us toward the King.

153-155 'Think about what's happened and we'll talk about it later.'

(*To Banquo*) Think upon what hath chanced and, at more time,
The interim having weighed it, let us speak
Our free hearts each to other.

BANQUO   Very gladly.   155

MACBETH   Till then, enough. Come, friends.

Exeunt

In this scene Duncan tells Macbeth and Banquo how impressed he is at the way they behaved in the battle. He makes Macbeth Thane of Cawdor and gives Banquo a hug.

ACT 1 SCENE 4
The royal palace at Forres
Flourish. Enter DUNCAN, MALCOLM,
DONALBAIN, LENNOX *and Attendants.*

1-2 'Has Cawdor been executed yet? Aren't the people who were given the job of killing him back yet?'
liege = lord

DUNCAN   Is execution done on Cawdor? Are not
Those in commission yet returned?

MALCOLM   My liege,
They are not yet come back. But I have spoke
With one that saw him die: who did report
That very frankly he confessed his treasons,   5
Implored your highness' pardon and set forth

7-11 'Nothing he did was as admirable as the way he died. He threw away the most precious thing he had (i.e. his life) as though it were worthless.'

A deep repentance. Nothing in his life
Became him like the leaving it; he died
As one that had been studied in his death
To throw away the dearest thing he owed,   10
As 'twere a careless trifle.

11-14 'There's no way of telling what someone thinks from their outward appearance — I trusted him completely.'

DUNCAN   There's no art
To find the mind's construction in the face:
He was a gentleman on whom I built
An absolute trust.

Enter MACBETH, BANQUO, ROSSE, *and* ANGUS

O worthiest cousin!
The sin of my ingratitude even now   15
Was heavy on me: thou art so far before
That swiftest wing of recompense is slow
To overtake thee. Would thou hadst less deserved,
That the proportion both of thanks and payment
Might have been mine: only I have left to say,   20
More is thy due than more than all can pay.

MACBETH   The service and the loyalty I owe,
In doing it, pays itself. Your highness' part
Is to receive our duties; and our duties
Are to your throne and state, children and servants,   25
Which do but what they should, by doing every thing
Safe toward your love and honour.

DUNCAN   Welcome hither.
I have begun to plant thee, and will labour
To make thee full of growing. Noble Banquo,
That hast no less deserved, nor must be known   30
No less to have done so, let me enfold thee
And hold thee to my heart.

BANQUO   There if I grow,
The harvest is your own.

DUNCAN   My plenteous joys,
Wanton in fulness, seek to hide themselves
In drops of sorrow. Sons, kinsmen, Thanes,   35
And you whose places are the nearest, know
We will establish our estate upon
Our eldest, Malcolm, whom we name hereafter
The Prince of Cumberland, which honour must
Not unaccompanied invest him only,   40
But signs of nobleness, like stars, shall shine
On all deservers. From hence to Inverness,
And bind us further to you.

MACBETH   The rest is labour, which is not used for you:
I'll be myself the harbinger and make joyful   45
The hearing of my wife with your approach.
So humbly take my leave.

DUNCAN   My worthy Cawdor!

MACBETH   *(Aside)* The Prince of Cumberland! That is a step
On which I must fall down, or else o'erleap,
For in my way it lies. Stars, hide your fires,   50
Let not light see my black and deep desires;
The eye wink at the hand. Yet let that be,
Which the eye fears, when it is done, to see.

Exit

DUNCAN   True, worthy Banquo; he is full so valiant,
And in his commendations I am fed;   55
It is a banquet to me. Let's after him,
Whose care is gone before to bid us welcome:
It is a peerless kinsman.

Flourish. Exeunt.

14-21 Duncan's saying "How can I ever repay you?" in about four different ways.

22-23 'Doing my duty for you is a reward in itself.'

26-27 'doing everything to make sure you're safe'

31-32 'let me give you a hug'

33-35 'I'm so disgustingly happy, that it makes me want to cry.'

36 'all my nearest and dearest'

37-42 'I'm making Malcolm my official heir, and Prince of Cumberland. And he won't be the only one to get a reward — there'll be titles for everyone who deserves them.'

42-43 'Let's go and stay at your place, so we can spend some time together.'

45-46 'I'll be the messenger myself, and go and make my wife happy by telling her you're coming to stay.'

48-53 'That puts a spanner in the works. I wish the stars would go out so there was no light to show the evil things I plan to do. I wish my eye could ignore what my hand is going to do.'

54-56 'Banquo, Macbeth is a top bloke. Let's get after him.'

peerless = the best

Act 1, Scene 4

8

The scene starts off with Lady Macbeth reading a letter from Macbeth, about what happened with the Witches. Then Macbeth arrives and they plot to kill Duncan.

ACT 1 SCENE 5
Macbeth's castle in Inverness

Enter LADY MACBETH *alone, with a letter.*

1-11 'On the day I won the battle I met the Witches. I've found out they know more than ordinary humans. I wanted them to tell me more but they vanished into thin air. Then messengers came from the King and called me the Thane of Cawdor — just what the Witches had called me before (when they said I'd be King too). I thought I'd let you know so you could enjoy thinking about what's coming your way.'

LADY MACBETH *(Reads)* "They met me in the day of success, and I have learned by the perfectest report they have more in them than mortal knowledge. When I burned in desire to question them further, they made themselves air, into which they vanished. Whiles I stood rapt in the wonder of it, came 5 missives from the King who all-hailed me Thane of Cawdor, by which title before these weïrd sisters saluted me and referred me to the coming on of time, with "Hail, King that shalt be." This have I thought good to deliver thee, my dearest partner of greatness, that thou mightst not lose the dues of rejoicing by 10 being ignorant of what greatness is promised thee. Lay it to thy heart, and farewell."

13-16 'You will be King, but I'm worried you're a bit too soft to sort it out.'

Glamis thou art, and Cawdor, and shalt be
What thou art promised; yet do I fear thy nature,
It is too full o'th'milk of human kindness 15
To catch the nearest way. Thou wouldst be great,
Art not without ambition, but without

18-20 'You want great things, but you don't want to do anything bad to get them. You won't cheat, but you wouldn't mind winning.'

The illness should attend it. What thou wouldst highly,
That wouldst thou holily; wouldst not play false,
And yet wouldst wrongly win. Thou'dst have, great Glamis, 20

20-23 'You want something you can only get one way — you don't mind getting it in that way, but you're afraid of actually doing the dirty deed.'

That which cries, 'Thus thou must do' if thou have it;
And that which rather thou dost fear to do,
Than wishest should be undone. Hie thee hither,
That I may pour my spirits in thine ear

23-28 She wants to talk all the goodness out of Macbeth — so nothing will hold him back from being King.

And chastise with the valour of my tongue 25
All that impedes thee from the golden round,
Which fate and metaphysical aid doth seem
To have thee crowned withal.

golden round = crown

metaphysical aid = supernatural help

Enter MESSENGER

28 'What's the news?'

What is your tidings?

MESSENGER The King comes here tonight.

29 'You're joking.' Lady Macbeth's confused because she was just thinking about Macbeth being King.

LADY MACBETH Thou'rt mad to say it.
Is not thy master with him? Who, were't so, 30
Would have informed for preparation.

30-31 'Isn't Macbeth with him? If the King was coming, Macbeth would've warned us.'

MESSENGER So please you, it is true: our thane is coming.
One of my fellows had the speed of him;
Who almost dead for breath, had scarcely more
Than would make up his message.

LADY MACBETH Give him tending, 35
He brings great news.

Exit MESSENGER

The raven himself is hoarse,
That croaks the fatal entrance of Duncan
Under my battlements. Come, you spirits

39-41 'I don't want to be a woman any more — fill me with cruelty.'

That tend on mortal thoughts, unsex me here
And fill me from the crown to the toe topfull 40
Of direst cruelty; make thick my blood,

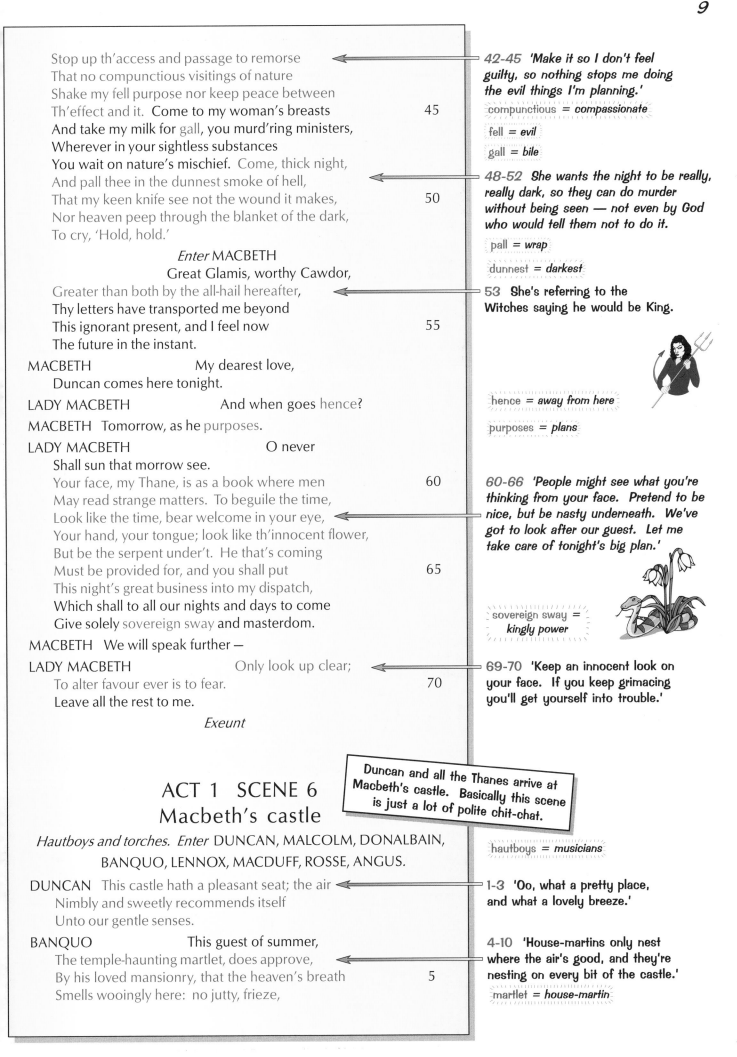

Stop up th'access and passage to remorse
That no compunctious visitings of nature
Shake my fell purpose nor keep peace between
Th'effect and it. Come to my woman's breasts   45
And take my milk for gall, you murd'ring ministers,
Wherever in your sightless substances
You wait on nature's mischief. Come, thick night,
And pall thee in the dunnest smoke of hell,
That my keen knife see not the wound it makes,   50
Nor heaven peep through the blanket of the dark,
To cry, 'Hold, hold.'

Enter MACBETH
                    Great Glamis, worthy Cawdor,
Greater than both by the all-hail hereafter,
Thy letters have transported me beyond
This ignorant present, and I feel now   55
The future in the instant.

MACBETH   My dearest love,
   Duncan comes here tonight.

LADY MACBETH   And when goes hence?

MACBETH Tomorrow, as he purposes.

LADY MACBETH   O never
   Shall sun that morrow see.
   Your face, my Thane, is as a book where men   60
   May read strange matters. To beguile the time,
   Look like the time, bear welcome in your eye,
   Your hand, your tongue; look like th'innocent flower,
   But be the serpent under't. He that's coming
   Must be provided for, and you shall put   65
   This night's great business into my dispatch,
   Which shall to all our nights and days to come
   Give solely sovereign sway and masterdom.

MACBETH We will speak further —

LADY MACBETH   Only look up clear;
   To alter favour ever is to fear.   70
   Leave all the rest to me.

Exeunt

ACT 1 SCENE 6
Macbeth's castle

Hautboys and torches. Enter DUNCAN, MALCOLM, DONALBAIN,
   BANQUO, LENNOX, MACDUFF, ROSSE, ANGUS.

DUNCAN This castle hath a pleasant seat; the air
   Nimbly and sweetly recommends itself
   Unto our gentle senses.

BANQUO   This guest of summer,
   The temple-haunting martlet, does approve,
   By his loved mansionry, that the heaven's breath   5
   Smells wooingly here: no jutty, frieze,

Side notes:

42-45 'Make it so I don't feel guilty, so nothing stops me doing the evil things I'm planning.'
compunctious = compassionate
fell = evil
gall = bile

48-52 She wants the night to be really, really dark, so they can do murder without being seen — not even by God who would tell them not to do it.
pall = wrap
dunnest = darkest

53 She's referring to the Witches saying he would be King.

hence = away from here
purposes = plans

60-66 'People might see what you're thinking from your face. Pretend to be nice, but be nasty underneath. We've got to look after our guest. Let me take care of tonight's big plan.'
sovereign sway = kingly power

69-70 'Keep an innocent look on your face. If you keep grimacing you'll get yourself into trouble.'

Duncan and all the Thanes arrive at Macbeth's castle. Basically this scene is just a lot of polite chit-chat.

hautboys = musicians

1-3 'Oo, what a pretty place, and what a lovely breeze.'

4-10 'House-martins only nest where the air's good, and they're nesting on every bit of the castle.'
martlet = house-martin

Buttress, nor coign of vantage, but this bird
Hath made his pendent bed and procreant cradle:
Where they most breed and haunt, I have observed,
The air is delicate.

Enter LADY MACBETH

DUNCAN   See, see, our honoured hostess!   10
The love that follows us sometime is our trouble,
Which still we thank as love. Herein I teach you
How you shall bid God yield us for your pains,
And thank us for your trouble.

14-18 'The trouble we've gone to is nothing compared to the rewards you've given us.'

LADY MACBETH   All our service
In every point twice done and then done double   15
Were poor and single business to contend
Against those honours deep and broad wherewith
Your majesty loads our house: for those of old,
And the late dignities heaped up to them,
We rest your hermits.

hermits = people who pray for others

coursed = chased

DUNCAN   Where's the Thane of Cawdor?   20
We coursed him at the heels, and had a purpose
To be his purveyor: but he rides well,
And his great love, sharp as his spur, hath holp him
To his home before us. Fair and noble hostess,
We are your guest to-night.

purveyor = someone who's job is to ride ahead and get things ready

holp = helped

25-28 'Your servants can have whatever they want — it's all yours really.'

LADY MACBETH   Your servants ever   25
Have theirs, themselves and what is theirs, in compt,
To make their audit at your highness' pleasure,
Still to return your own.

DUNCAN   Give me your hand;
Conduct me to mine host: we love him highly,
And shall continue our graces towards him.   30
By your leave, hostess.

Exeunt

At first Macbeth decides against killing Duncan — he's not sure he'll get away with it, and thinks Duncan is a good man. Then Lady Macbeth says they can make it look as if Duncan was killed by his servants. Macbeth agrees to the plan.

ACT 1 SCENE 7
Macbeth's castle. Near the hall.

Hautboys. Torches. Enter a butler and many servants with dishes and service over the stage. Then enter MACBETH.

2-7 'If I could be sure the murder wouldn't bring me any bad consequences, I'd do it and not worry about the future.'

MACBETH If it were done when 'tis done, then 'twere well
It were done quickly. If th'assassination
Could trammel up the consequence and catch
With his surcease, success, that but this blow
Might be the be-all and the end-all — here,   5
But here, upon this bank and shoal of time,
We'd jump the life to come. But in these cases,
We still have judgement here that we but teach
Bloody instructions, which being taught, return
To plague th'inventor. This even-handed justice   10
Commends th'ingredience of our poisoned chalice
To our own lips. He's here in double trust:
First, as I am his kinsman and his subject,
Strong both against the deed; then, as his host,

surcease = death

7-10 'People who commit murder set an example for others. Murderers get murdered.'

12-14 'I shouldn't kill Duncan because I'm a relative and he's my king, and because I'm his host'

Who should against his murderer shut the door,   15
Not bear the knife myself. Besides, this Duncan
Hath borne his faculties so meek, hath been
So clear in his great office, that his virtues
Will plead like angels, trumpet-tongued against
The deep damnation of his taking-off.   20
And pity, like a naked newborn babe
Striding the blast, or heaven's cherubin horsed
Upon the sightless couriers of the air,
Shall blow the horrid deed in every eye,
That tears shall drown the wind. I have no spur   25
To prick the sides of my intent, but only
Vaulting ambition which o'erleaps itself
And falls on th'other —

Enter LADY MACBETH
How now? What news?

LADY MACBETH   He has almost supped. Why have you left the
                                                        chamber?

MACBETH   Hath he asked for me?

LADY MACBETH   Know you not he has?   30

MACBETH   We will proceed no further in this business.
He hath honoured me of late, and I have bought
Golden opinions from all sorts of people,
Which would be worn now in their newest gloss,
Not cast aside so soon.

LADY MACBETH   Was the hope drunk   35
Wherein you dressed yourself? Hath it slept since?
And wakes it now to look so green and pale
At what it did so freely? From this time,
Such I account thy love. Art thou afeard
To be the same in thine own act and valour,   40
As thou art in desire? Wouldst thou have that
Which thou esteem'st the ornament of life,
And live a coward in thine own esteem,
Letting I dare not wait upon I would,
Like the poor cat i'th'adage?

MACBETH   Prithee, peace.   45
I dare do all that may become a man;
Who dares do more is none.

LADY MACBETH   What beast was't then
That made you break this enterprise to me?
When you durst do it, then you were a man.
And to be more than what you were, you would   50
Be so much more the man. Nor time, nor place
Did then adhere, and yet you would make both.
They have made themselves and that their fitness now
Does unmake you. I have given suck and know
How tender 'tis to love the babe that milks me: 55
I would, while it was smiling in my face,
Have plucked my nipple from his boneless gums
And dashed the brains out, had I so sworn
As you have done to this.

Margin notes:

16-20 He also shouldn't kill Duncan because he's been a good king.

Oops, pardon me.

21-25 'Pity (like a baby or an angel riding on the wind) will take the dreadful deed and blow it so hard that it will bring tears to people's eyes — enough tears to drown the wind itself.'

25-28 'I've got no real desire to kill Duncan. I'm just ambitious but that won't make me do it.'

29 'He's almost finished eating. Why've you left the room?'

31-35 'We're not going through with it. Duncan's been kind to me and everyone thinks I'm great. We should be making the most of it, not throwing it away.'

35-38 She's saying Macbeth's acting like he was drunk when he agreed to the plan. Now he's slept it off and feels a bit hungover, he's not so sure.

38-39 'If you won't do it, then I don't reckon you love me much.'

39-43 'Are you too scared to do what you dream of doing? It seems like you want something, but you're too cowardly to take it.'

45 The cat wanted to eat fish, but didn't want to get its feet wet.
adage = proverb
may become = is suitable for

47-48 'What monster made you tell me all about this in the first place then?'
durst = dared

51-59 'It wasn't the right time or place then, but now that it is, you've turned chicken. I've breastfed a baby and, even though I loved that baby, if I'd promised you that I'd kill it, I'd go through with it.'

MACBETH   If we should fail?

LADY MACBETH   We fail?

60 *'Make yourself feel really brave.'*

But screw your courage to the sticking-place,   60
And we'll not fail. When Duncan is asleep,

62-3 *'He'll easily fall asleep 'cos he's had a tiring journey today.'*

Whereto the rather shall his day's hard journey
Soundly invite him, his two chamberlains

63-72 *'I'll get Duncan's servants drunk so they don't know what's going on, and when they're asleep we can do what we like to Duncan, and blame everything on the servants.'*

Will I with wine and wassail so convince
That memory, the warder of the brain,   65
Shall be a fume, and the receipt of reason
A limbeck only. When in swinish sleep
Their drenchèd natures lie as in a death,
What cannot you and I perform upon
Th'unguarded Duncan? What not put upon   70
His spongy officers, who shall bear the guilt
Of our great quell?

wassail = toasts (e.g. 'cheers')

convince = overpower

quell = murder

72-74 *'You should only have sons, 'cos you're well 'ard.'*

MACBETH   Bring forth men-children only,
For thy undaunted mettle should compose
Nothing but males. Will it not be received,

74-77 *'Everyone'll think that the servants killed Duncan when we've put blood on them and used their daggers, won't they?'*

When we have marked with blood those sleepy two   75
Of his own chamber and used their very daggers,
That they have done't?

77-79 *'Who'd dare to think anything else, 'cos we'll go on about how sad we are that Duncan's dead?'*

LADY MACBETH   Who dares receive it other,
As we shall make our griefs and clamour roar
Upon his death?

79-82 *'I'm convinced. I'll put all my effort into it. Go and pretend to be all nice, so people won't know what you're thinking.'*

MACBETH   I am settled and bend up
Each corporal agent to this terrible feat.   80
Away, and mock the time with fairest show,
False face must hide what the false heart doth know.

corporal agent = body part

Exeunt

Gulp

Act 1 — Revision Summary

If you don't know the play in detail, you <u>can't</u> write detailed, high-scoring essays. To test whether you really understand what's going on, and what all that prehistoric poetry is babbling on about, have a go at these questions. At first you'll have to look back through Act 1 to get some of the answers, but after a few goes you should be able to do them all off the top of your head.

1) In <u>Act1, Scene 1</u>, where do the witches agree to meet up with Macbeth?

2) Who are Graymalkin and Paddock?

3) What does "anon" mean? a) anonymous, b) coming, c) no

4) In <u>Act1, Scene 2</u>, why does Duncan call the Captain "bloody"?

5) Rewrite this sentence in modern English: "He can report/ As seemeth by his plight, of the revolt/ The newest state."

6) Write down the exact words the Captain uses to describe the two sides in the battle in the speech starting at line 7 of Scene 2, and then rewrite them in modern English.

7) Who do "the multiplying villainies of nature" swarm upon in line 11? What does this mean?

8) What would you be doing if you "unseamed" somebody from "the nave to the chops"?

9) Describe the events of the battle in your own words.

10) In <u>Act 1, Scene 3</u> what does the First Witch say she's been doing? What does the Second Witch say she's been doing?

11) Why can't Banquo quite believe the witches are female?

12) What three titles do the witches greet Macbeth with? Which ones has he already got?

13) Quote the words Banquo says that tell you how Macbeth reacts to the witches.

14) How would you say "Thou shalt get kings, though thou be none," in modern English?

15) Who gives Macbeth the official news about his new title?

16) What physical reactions does Macbeth describe in lines 134-136?

17) Does "without my stir" mean:
   a) without me doing anything, or
   b) without creating a fuss?

18) In <u>Act 1, Scene 4</u>, which words tell you that Duncan is surprised that the old Thane of Cawdor turned out to be bad?

19) Macbeth says to Duncan, "The service and the loyalty I owe,/ In doing it, pays itself." Do you think he means it? Why?

20) Rewrite these words in modern English: "let me enfold thee and hold thee to my heart". Who says them, and who does he say them to?

21) Who's the new Prince of Cumberland? Write down the words that show Macbeth thinks that's a problem.

22) In Lady Macbeth's speech at the beginning of <u>Act 1, Scene 5</u>, she says Macbeth "shalt be what thou art promised". What does she mean? Why does she think it might not happen?

23) What part of the body does 'Glamis' rhyme with?

24) Why does Lady Macbeth want to be 'unsexed'?

25) What does Lady Macbeth warn Macbeth to do in lines 60-64?

26) In <u>Act 1, Scene 6</u>, does Duncan seem pleased to be at Glamis?

27) At the beginning of <u>Act 1, Scene 7</u> Macbeth wants to back out of the plan to kill Duncan. By the end he's changed his mind again. What words tell you he has decided to kill Duncan?

28) What's Lady Macbeth's plan for bumping off Duncan?

29) Translate "screw your courage to the sticking place" into normal English.

30) Write down 5 quotes from Act 1 that show people think Macbeth is brave, and 5 quotes that show he is feeling frightened or confused.

This is the scene with the famous 'dagger' speech. At the beginning, Banquo talks to Macbeth about the Witches' predictions. After he's gone, Macbeth sees the dagger, goes on a bit, then heads off to kill Duncan.

ACT 2 SCENE 1
Courtyard in Macbeth's castle

Enter BANQUO, *and* FLEANCE *bearing a torch before him*

BANQUO How goes the night, boy?

FLEANCE The moon is down; I have not heard the clock.

3 'The moon goes down at 12 o'clock.' ⟶ BANQUO And she goes down at twelve.

4 'It must be later then, Dad.' ⟶ FLEANCE I take't, 'tis later, sir.

BANQUO Hold, take my sword. There's husbandry in heaven. 5
    Their candles are all out. Take thee that too.

7-8 'I feel dead tired but I don't want to sleep.' ⟶ A heavy summons lies like lead upon me,

8-10 'Good spirits, stop me thinking horrible thoughts that'll turn into nightmares if I sleep.' ⟶ And yet I would not sleep: merciful powers,
    Restrain in me the cursèd thoughts that nature
    Gives way to in repose!

You and me, Banquo, we're real pals...

Enter MACBETH, *and a* SERVANT *with a torch*
                    Give me my sword. 10
    Who's there?

MACBETH A friend.

13-17 'Aren't you in bed yet? The King is. He's been dead happy and given you some great stuff, like this diamond for your wife.' ⟶ BANQUO What, sir, not yet at rest? The king's abed.
    He hath been in unusual pleasure, and
    Sent forth great largess to your offices. 15
    This diamond he greets your wife withal,

17-18 'Duncan ended the day all happy.' ⟶ By the name of most kind hostess; and shut up
    In measureless content.

18-20 'Because we weren't prepared, we couldn't do as much (for Duncan) as we would've liked.' ⟶ MACBETH   Being unprepared,
    Our will became the servant to defect,
    Which else should free have wrought.

BANQUO   All's well. 20

21-22 i.e. the Witches' prediction about being Thane of Cawdor came true ⟶ I dreamt last night of the three weïrd sisters —
    To you they have showed some truth.

22 He's lying! ⟶ MACBETH   I think not of them:

23-25 'When we can spare an hour, let's talk about that stuff, if you have the time.' ⟶ Yet, when we can entreat an hour to serve,
    We would spend it in some words upon that business,
    If you would grant the time.

BANQUO   At your kind'st leisure. 25

26-27 'If you follow my advice when the time comes, it'll be to your advantage.' ⟶ MACBETH If you shall cleave to my consent, when 'tis,
    It shall make honour for you.

27-30 'So long as I don't lose any honour by trying to get more, and keep my conscience clear, I'll follow your advice.' This last bit suggests Banquo is a bit suspicious about what Macbeth is intending to do. ⟶ BANQUO   So I lose none
    In seeking to augment it, but still keep
    My bosom franchised and allegiance clear,
    I shall be counselled.

MACBETH   Good repose the while! 30

good repose = sleep well

BANQUO Thanks, sir — the like to you!

Exeunt BANQUO *and* FLEANCE

MACBETH Go bid thy mistress, when my drink is ready,
    She strike upon the bell. Get thee to bed.

Exit SERVANT

Once the Servant has left the stage, Macbeth is on his own. ⟶ Is this a dagger which I see before me,
    The handle toward my hand? Come, let me clutch thee. 35

I have thee not, and yet I see thee still.
Art thou not, fatal vision, sensible
To feeling as to sight? Or art thou but
A dagger of the mind, a false creation,
Proceeding from the heat-oppressèd brain?   40
I see thee yet, in form as palpable
As this which now I draw.
Thou marshall'st me the way that I was going,
And such an instrument I was to use.
Mine eyes are made the fools o' the other senses,   45
Or else worth all the rest. I see thee still,
And on thy blade and dudgeon gouts of blood,
Which was not so before. There's no such thing —
It is the bloody business which informs
Thus to mine eyes. Now o'er the one halfworld   50
Nature seems dead, and wicked dreams abuse
The curtained sleep. Now witchcraft celebrates
Pale Hecate's offerings, and withered murder,
Alarumed by his sentinel, the wolf,
Whose howl's his watch, thus with his stealthy pace.   55
With Tarquin's ravishing strides, towards his design
Moves like a ghost. Thou sure and firm-set earth,
Hear not my steps, which way they walk, for fear
Thy very stones prate of my whereabout,
And take the present horror from the time,   60
Which now suits with it. Whiles I threat, he lives —
Words to the heat of deeds too cold breath gives.

A bell rings

I go, and it is done; the bell invites me.
Hear it not, Duncan; for it is a knell
That summons thee to heaven or to hell.   65

Exit

I have thee not = *I can't hold the dagger*

37-38 *'Can't you be touched as well as seen?'*

palpable = *solid*

42 *Macbeth gets his own dagger out.*

43-44 *The imaginary dagger is pointing him to Duncan's room, and is like the one he was going to use to kill Duncan.*

45-46 *'Either my eyes are rubbish, or they're better than all my other senses put together.'*

47 *'On the blade and handle there are drops of blood.'*

bloody business = *plan to murder Duncan*

50-53 *'It's night over half the world, and nightmares disturb sleep. Witches are making ritual offerings to Hecate (goddess of witches).'*

53-57 *He talks about "murder" as if it's a person, who's been alerted by his guard dog, and is walking silently toward his victim.*

57-59 *'I hope no one hears my footsteps.'*

64-65 *'Duncan, you're gonna die.'*

knell = *ring of a funeral bell*

ACT 2 SCENE 2
Courtyard in Macbeth's castle
Enter LADY MACBETH

Lady Macbeth has got Duncan's servants drunk. Macbeth enters. He's just killed Duncan, and feeling a tad guilty about it. Lady Macbeth tells him to pull himself together. She smears blood on the sleeping servants to pin the deed on them.

LADY MACBETH   That which hath made them drunk hath made me
                                                        bold;
What hath quenched them hath given me fire. Hark! Peace!
It was the owl that shrieked, the fatal bellman,
Which gives the stern'st good-night. He is about it:
The doors are open, and the surfeited grooms   5
Do mock their charge with snores — I have drugged their possets,
That death and nature do contend about them,
Whether they live or die.

MACBETH   *(Within)*   Who's there? what, ho!

LADY MACBETH   Alack, I am afraid they have awaked,
And 'tis not done. The attempt and not the deed   10
Confounds us. Hark! I laid their daggers ready;
He could not miss 'em. Had he not resembled
My father as he slept, I had done't.

1-2 *She's given the servants something to make them drunk, and has had a bit herself to make her brave.*

bellman = *bellringer at a funeral*

4 *Macbeth is doing the deed.*

5-6 *The servants are snoring, which makes a joke of their responsibilities.*

posset = *a kind of drink*

9-11 *She's worried that Macbeth hasn't done it and their plot will be found out.*

12-13 *'I would have done it if he didn't look my Dad.'*

16

Enter MACBETH

My husband!

MACBETH I have done the deed. Didst thou not hear a noise?

LADY MACBETH I heard the owl scream and the crickets cry.   15
Did not you speak?

MACBETH   When?

LADY MACBETH   Now.

MACBETH   As I descended?

LADY MACBETH Ay.

MACBETH Hark!
Who lies i' the second chamber?

LADY MACBETH   Donalbain.

MACBETH *(Looking at his hands)* This is a sorry sight.   20

LADY MACBETH A foolish thought, to say a sorry sight.

MACBETH There's one did laugh in's sleep, and one cried 'Murder!'
That they did wake each other — I stood, and heard them,
But they did say their prayers, and addressed them
Again to sleep.

LADY MACBETH There are two lodged together.   25

MACBETH One cried 'God bless us!' and 'Amen' the other,
As they had seen me with these hangman's hands.
List'ning their fear, I could not say 'Amen'
When they did say 'God bless us.'

LADY MACBETH Consider it not so deeply.   30

MACBETH But wherefore could not I pronounce 'Amen'?
I had most need of blessing and 'Amen'
Stuck in my throat.

LADY MACBETH These deeds must not be thought
After these ways; so, it will make us mad.

MACBETH Methought I heard a voice cry, 'Sleep no more,   35
Macbeth does murder sleep', the innocent sleep,
Sleep that knits up the ravelled sleeve of care,
The death of each day's life, sore labour's bath,
Balm of hurt minds, great nature's second course,
Chief nourisher in life's feast.

LADY MACBETH   What do you mean?   40

MACBETH Still it cried, 'Sleep no more' to all the house,
'Glamis hath murdered sleep', and therefore Cawdor
Shall sleep no more — Macbeth shall sleep no more.

LADY MACBETH Who was it, that thus cried? Why, worthy thane,
You do unbend your noble strength to think   45
So brain-sickly of things. Go get some water
And wash this filthy witness from your hand.
Why did you bring these daggers from the place?
They must lie there. Go carry them and smear
The sleepy servants with blood.

MACBETH   I'll go no more.   50
I am afraid to think what I have done —
Look on't again, I dare not.

---

descended = came down

25 'Malcolm and Donalbain are both sleeping in the next room.'

27 'As if they'd seen my bloody hands.'
28-29 When Malcolm and Donalbain said "God bless" Macbeth couldn't say "Amen". He feels too evil to say prayers.

30 'Stop stressing about it.'

33-34 'Don't think about it or we'll go crazy.'

35-36 This is either a supernatural voice, or just Macbeth's own mind.

37-40 'Sleep keeps the mind in working order' — he's upset that the voice said he wouldn't sleep any more.

Glamis = Cawdor = Macbeth

45-46 'You make yourself weak thinking such weird things.'
witness = evidence

49-50 It'll make people think the servants killed Duncan.

50-52 'I'm not going back. It scares me to think of what I've done — I'm not brave enough to look at it again.'

Act 2, Scene 2

LADY MACBETH   Infirm of purpose! ⟵

   Give me the daggers. The sleeping and the dead ⟵

   Are but as pictures; 'tis the eye of childhood

   That fears a painted devil. If he do bleed,   55

   I'll gild the faces of the servants withal, ⟵

   For it must seem their guilt.

           Exit. Knock within.

MACBETH   Whence is that knocking? ⟵

   How is't with me, when every noise appals me?

   What hands are here? Ha — they pluck out mine eyes.

   Will all great Neptune's ocean wash this blood   60

   Clean from my hand? No — this my hand will rather

   The multitudinous seas incarnadine,

   Making the green one red.

          Enter LADY MACBETH

LADY MACBETH My hands are of your colour, but I shame

   To wear a heart so white.

          Knock within

         I hear a knocking   65

   At the south entry. Retire we to our chamber; ⟵

   A little water clears us of this deed. ⟵

   How easy is it then! Your constancy ⟵

   Hath left you unattended.

          Knock within

         Hark, more knocking.

   Get on your night-gown, lest occasion call us   70 ⟵

   And show us to be watchers. Be not lost

   So poorly in your thoughts.

MACBETH To know my deed, 'twere best not know myself. ⟵

          Knock within

   Wake Duncan with thy knocking: I would thou couldst. ⟵

          Exeunt

ACT 2 SCENE 3
The entrance to Macbeth's castle

Enter a PORTER. *Knocking within.*

PORTER Here's a knocking indeed — if a man were porter of ⟵

   hell-gate, he should have old turning the key. *(Knock)*

   Knock, knock,knock. Who's there i'th'name of Beelzebub?

   Here's a farmer that hanged himself on th'expectation ⟵

   of plenty. Come in time — have napkins enough about you, 5

   here you'll sweat for't. *(Knock)* Knock, knock. Who's there

   in th'other devil's name? Faith, here's an equivocator that ⟵

   could swear in both the scales against either scale, who

   committed treason enough for God's sake, yet could not

   equivocate to heaven. O, come in, equivocator. *(Knock)* 10

   Knock, knock, knock. Who's there? Faith, here's an English

   tailor come hither for stealing out of a French hose. Come in,

   tailor, here you may roast your goose, *(Knock)* Knock, knock.

Side notes:

52 'Wimp!'

53-54 'Dead people are nothing to be scared of.'

56-57 'I'll paint the servants' faces with Duncan's blood, to make them look guilty.'

57-63 'Where's that knocking coming from? Why am I scared of every noise? What are these hands? I can't stand looking at them. Would all the world's oceans wash the blood off my hands? Nope, instead my hand would turn the ocean red.'

incarnadine = turn red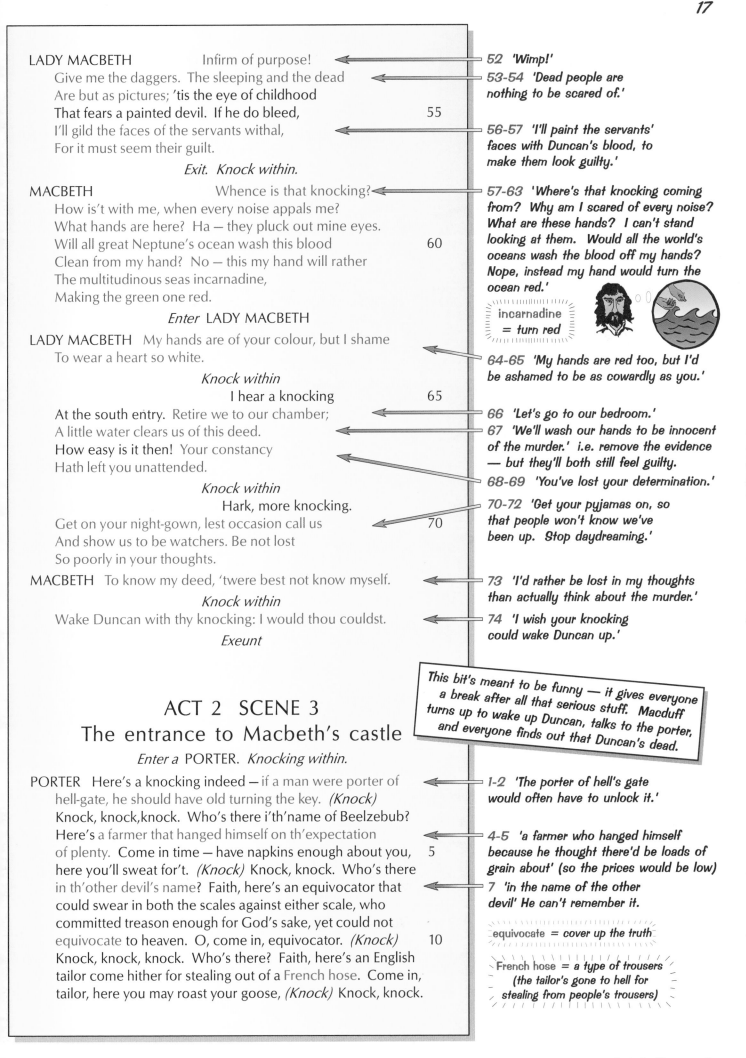

64-65 'My hands are red too, but I'd be ashamed to be as cowardly as you.'

66 'Let's go to our bedroom.'

67 'We'll wash our hands to be innocent of the murder.' i.e. remove the evidence — but they'll both still feel guilty.

68-69 'You've lost your determination.'

70-72 'Get your pyjamas on, so that people won't know we've been up. Stop daydreaming.'

73 'I'd rather be lost in my thoughts than actually think about the murder.'

74 'I wish your knocking could wake Duncan up.'

This bit's meant to be funny — it gives everyone a break after all that serious stuff. Macduff turns up to wake up Duncan, talks to the porter, and everyone finds out that Duncan's dead.

1-2 'The porter of hell's gate would often have to unlock it.'

4-5 'a farmer who hanged himself because he thought there'd be loads of grain about' (so the prices would be low)

7 'in the name of the other devil' He can't remember it.

equivocate = cover up the truth

French hose = a type of trousers (the tailor's gone to hell for stealing from people's trousers) the primrose way to th'everlasting bonfire = the pleasant path that leads to hell

remember the porter = give me a tip

Never at quiet — what are you? But this place is too cold for hell. I'll devil-porter it no further — I had thought to have let   15
in some of all professions that go the primrose way to
th'everlasting bonfire. *(Knock)* Anon, anon! I pray you,
remember the porter. *(Opens door)*

Enter MACDUFF *and* LENOX

MACDUFF Was it so late, friend, ere you went to bed,
That you do lie so late?   20

21-22 'Yes, we were partying until morning, and boozing gives you three things.'

PORTER Faith, sir, we were carousing till the second cock, and
drink, sir, is a great provoker of three things.

MACDUFF What three things does drink especially provoke?

nose-painting = makes your nose go red

25-26 'Drink makes you want sex, but also makes you unable to perform.'

equivocator = two-faced liar

PORTER Marry, sir, nose-painting, sleep, and urine. Lechery, sir,
it provokes, and unprovokes — it provokes the desire, but it   25
takes away the performance. Therefore much drink may be
said to be an equivocator with lechery — it makes him, and it
mars him, it sets him on, and it takes him off, it persuades
him and disheartens him, makes him stand to and not stand
to. In conclusion, equivocates him in a sleep, and, giving   30
him the lie, leaves him.

MACDUFF I believe drink gave thee the lie last night.

33-35 'The drink got me tight in the throat (i.e. made me sick), but I got him by the legs and threw him out (i.e. vomited).'

PORTER That it did, sir, i'the very throat on me, but I requited
him for his lie, and, I think, being too strong for him, though
he took up my legs sometime, yet I made a shift to cast him.   35

Enter MACBETH

stirring = waking

MACDUFF Is thy master stirring?
Our knocking has awaked him — here he comes.

Exit PORTER

LENOX Good morrow, noble sir.

MACBETH   Good morrow, both.

MACDUFF Is the King stirring, worthy Thane?

MACBETH   Not yet.

slipped = missed

MACDUFF He did command me to call timely on him,   40
I have almost slipped the hour.

MACBETH   I'll bring you to him.

MACDUFF I know this is a joyful trouble to you, but yet 'tis one.

43 'It's worth the effort because it's such a pleasure.'

MACBETH The labour we delight in physics pain.
This is the door.

MACDUFF   I'll make so bold to call,
For 'tis my limited service.

Exit   45

46 'Is the king leaving today?'

LENOX Goes the King hence today?

appoint so = plan to

MACBETH   He does — he did appoint so.

47-52 It was a really stormy night.

LENOX The night has been unruly — where we lay,
Our chimneys were blown down, and, as they say,
Lamentings heard i'th'air, strange screams of death
And prophesying with accents terrible   50
Of dire combustion and confused events,
New hatched to th'woeful time. The obscure bird

52-53 'The owl was hooting all night long.'

Clamoured the livelong night. Some say, the earth

Was feverous and did shake.

MACBETH   'Twas a rough night.

LENOX   My young remembrance cannot parallel   55
    A fellow to it.

55-56 'I can't remember one so bad.'

                Enter MACDUFF

MACDUFF   O horror! horror! horror!
    Tongue nor heart cannot conceive, nor name thee.

57 'I can't believe it or say it.'

MACBETH *and* LENOX   What's the matter?

MACDUFF   Confusion now hath made his masterpiece.
    Most sacrilegious murder hath broke ope   60
    The Lord's anointed temple and stole thence
    The life o'th'building.

60-62 'Murder has opened Duncan's body and taken his life.'

MACBETH   What is't you say, the life?

64 'Go to Duncan's room.'

LENOX   Mean you his majesty?

MACDUFF   Approach the chamber and destroy your sight
    With a new Gorgon.   Do not bid me speak —   65
    See and then speak yourselves.

64-65 The Gorgon was a woman so ugly that anyone who looked at her turned to stone.

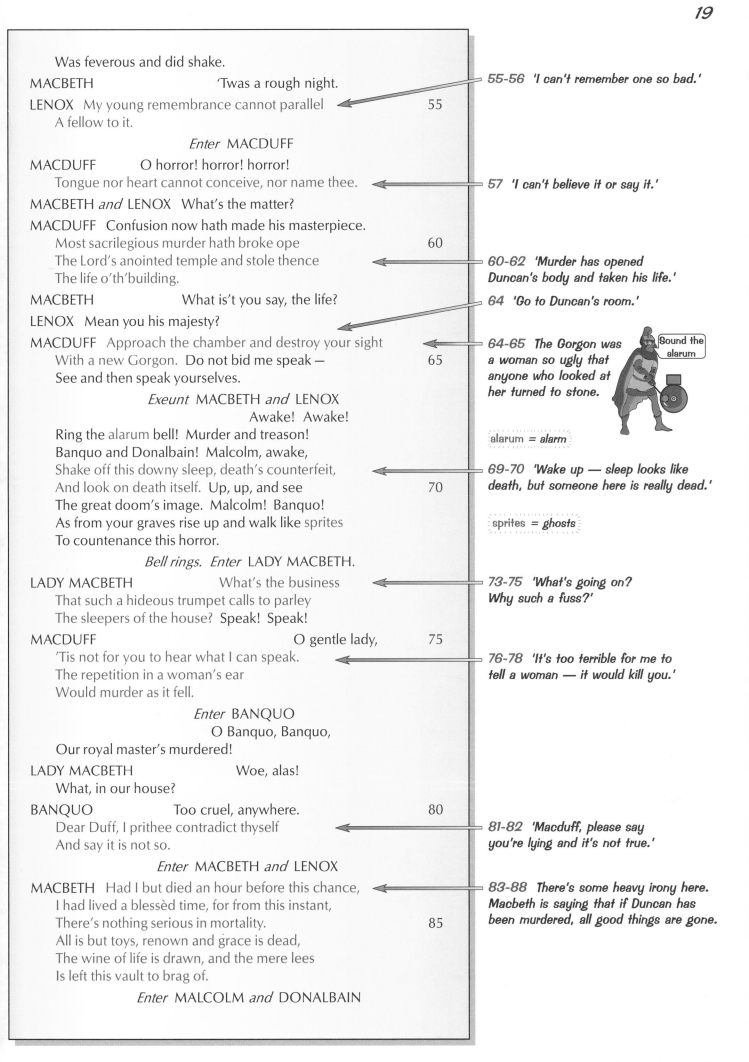

Sound the alarum

alarum = alarm

         Exeunt MACBETH *and* LENOX
            Awake! Awake!
    Ring the alarum bell! Murder and treason!
    Banquo and Donalbain! Malcolm, awake,
    Shake off this downy sleep, death's counterfeit,
    And look on death itself.   Up, up, and see   70
    The great doom's image. Malcolm! Banquo!
    As from your graves rise up and walk like sprites
    To countenance this horror.

69-70 'Wake up — sleep looks like death, but someone here is really dead.'

sprites = ghosts

      Bell rings. Enter LADY MACBETH.

LADY MACBETH   What's the business
    That such a hideous trumpet calls to parley
    The sleepers of the house? Speak! Speak!

73-75 'What's going on? Why such a fuss?'

MACDUFF   O gentle lady,   75
    'Tis not for you to hear what I can speak.
    The repetition in a woman's ear
    Would murder as it fell.

76-78 'It's too terrible for me to tell a woman — it would kill you.'

          Enter BANQUO
          O Banquo, Banquo,
    Our royal master's murdered!

LADY MACBETH   Woe, alas!
    What, in our house?

BANQUO   Too cruel, anywhere.   80
    Dear Duff, I prithee contradict thyself
    And say it is not so.

81-82 'Macduff, please say you're lying and it's not true.'

       Enter MACBETH *and* LENOX

MACBETH   Had I but died an hour before this chance,
    I had lived a blessèd time, for from this instant,
    There's nothing serious in mortality.   85
    All is but toys, renown and grace is dead,
    The wine of life is drawn, and the mere lees
    Is left this vault to brag of.

83-88 There's some heavy irony here. Macbeth is saying that if Duncan has been murdered, all good things are gone.

      Enter MALCOLM *and* DONALBAIN

DONALBAIN What is amiss?

MACBETH   You are, and do not know't.
The spring, the head, the fountain of your blood   90
Is stopped, the very source of it is stopped.

MACDUFF Your royal father's murdered.

MALCOLM   O, by whom?

LENOX Those of his chamber, as it seemed, had done't.
Their hands and faces were all badged with blood,
So were their daggers which, unwiped, we found   95
Upon their pillows. They stared and were distracted,
No man's life was to be trusted with them.

MACBETH O, yet I do repent me of my fury
That I did kill them.

MACDUFF   Wherefore did you so?

MACBETH Who can be wise, amazed, temperate, and furious,   100
Loyal and neutral, in a moment? No man.
Th'expedition of my violent love
Outran the pauser, reason. Here lay Duncan,
His silver skin laced with his golden blood
And his gashed stabs looked like a breach in nature,   105
For ruin's wasteful entrance. There, the murderers,
Steeped in the colours of their trade, their daggers
Unmannerly breeched with gore. Who could refrain,
That had a heart to love, and in that heart
Courage to make's love known?

LADY MACBETH   Help me hence, ho!   110

MACDUFF Look to the lady.

MALCOLM *(To Donalbain)* Why do we hold our tongues,
That most may claim this argument for ours?

DONALBAIN *(To Malcolm)* What should be spoken here,
Where our fate hid in an auger hole may rush
And seize us? Let's away. Our tears are not yet brewed.   115

MALCOLM Nor our strong sorrow upon the foot of motion.

BANQUO Look to the lady,
                LADY MACBETH *is taken out*
And when we have our naked frailties hid
That suffer in exposure, let us meet,
And question this most bloody piece of work   120
To know it further. Fears and scruples shake us —
In the great hand of God I stand and thence
Against the undivulged pretence I fight
Of treasonous malice.

MACDUFF   And so do I.

ALL   So all.

MACBETH Let's briefly put on manly readiness   125
And meet i'th'hall together.

ALL   Well contented.
                Exeunt all but MALCOLM *and* DONALBAIN

MALCOLM What will you do? Let's not consort with them.

---

89 'What's wrong?'

90-91 'Your Dad's dead.'

93-96 'I reckon it was his servants — they were covered in blood and so were their daggers, which they hadn't even wiped.'

98-99 'Sorry — I killed the servants.'

100-108 'I flipped out when I saw Duncan dead. I saw the murderers (the servants) covered in blood, and their bloody daggers.'

108-110 'Anyone who genuinely loved Duncan would have done the same.' This is a really over the top speech — he's trying to convince everyone.

110 Lady Macbeth is fainting.

111-112 'Why don't we say something? Everyone else is saying what we should be saying.'

113-115 'No, we might be murdered next, let's get out of here.'
auger hole = hole made by tiny drill

116 'We're not ready to show how sad we are yet.'

118-124 'Let's get dressed, then we can think about what's happened. I'm willing to do whatever God wants.'

125 'Let's get ready quickly.'

well contented = agreed

127 'What are you going to do? I don't think we should meet with them.'

Act 2, Scene 3

To show an unfelt sorrow is an office
Which the false man does easy. I'll to England.

DONALBAIN   To Ireland, I. Our separated fortune   130
Shall keep us both the safer. Where we are,
There's daggers in men's smiles, the nea'er in blood,
The nearer bloody.

MALCOLM   This murderous shaft that's shot
Hath not yet lighted, and our safest way
Is to avoid the aim. Therefore to horse,   135
And let us not be dainty of leave-taking,
But shift away. There's warrant in that theft
Which steals itself when there's no mercy left.

Exeunt

128-129 *'Evil men find it easy to pretend to be upset when they're not. I'm off to England.'*

130-133 *'I'll go to Ireland. We'll be safer apart. We can't trust people here.'*

133-135 *'Something bad's going to happen — the best way to avoid it is not to be here.'*

136-138 *'It's safer to leave straight away. Stealing away is a type of stealing that's OK.'*

ACT 2 SCENE 4
Outside Macbeth's castle
Enter ROSSE *and an* OLD MAN.

Rosse and a random old man gossip about the weird things that have been happening since Duncan's death. Macduff arrives and says that it looks as though Malcolm and Donalbain are the ones who had Duncan killed, because they've scarpered — so Macbeth will be King now.

OLD MAN   Threescore and ten I can remember well:
Within the volume of which time I have seen
Hours dreadful and things strange, but this sore night
Hath trifled former knowings.

ROSSE   Ah, good father,
Thou seest, the heavens, as troubled with man's act,   5
Threaten his bloody stage — by the clock, 'tis day,
And yet dark night strangles the travelling lamp.
Is't night's predominance, or the day's shame,
That darkness does the face of earth entomb,
When living light should kiss it?

OLD MAN   'Tis unnatural,   10
Even like the deed that's done. On Tuesday last,
A falcon, towering in her pride of place,
Was by a mousing owl hawked at and killed.

ROSSE   And Duncan's horses — a thing most strange and certain —
Beauteous and swift, the minions of their race,   15
Turned wild in nature, broke their stalls, flung out,
Contending 'gainst obedience, as they would make
War with mankind.

OLD MAN   'Tis said they eat each other.

ROSSE   They did so, to the amazement of mine eyes
That looked upon't. Here comes the good Macduff.   20

Enter MACDUFF
How goes the world, sir, now?

MACDUFF   Why, see you not?

ROSSE   Is't known who did this more than bloody deed?

MACDUFF   Those that Macbeth hath slain.

ROSSE   Alas, the day!
What good could they pretend?

1-4 *'I've been alive for 70 years: I've seen some bad things in that time, but this dreadful night has made everything else seem trivial.'*

4-10 *'You see, old man, the sky's dark as though it's angry about events on earth. The clock says it's day but there's no sun. It's as if night has taken over, or day is hiding away — it's dark when it should be light.'*

travelling lamp = sun

10-20 *They talk about the strange things that have been happening since Duncan was killed, such as Duncan's horses eating each other (hmmm...).*

minions = *favourites*

22 *'Do they know who killed Duncan yet?'*

23 *'It was the servants that Macbeth killed.'*

24 *'Why did they do it?'*

24-27 'They were ordered to do it.
Malcolm and Donalbain have run away,
so they're prime suspects.'

MACDUFF   They were suborned:
Malcolm and Donalbain, the king's two sons,   25
Are stol'n away and fled, which puts upon them
Suspicion of the deed.

27-30 'It's not natural! Greedy
ambition has led them to kill their
own flesh and blood. Looks like
Macbeth will be King now, then.'

ROSSE   'Gainst nature still!
Thriftless ambition, that wilt ravin up
Thine own life's means! Then 'tis most like
The sovereignty will fall upon Macbeth.   30

sovereignty = job of King

31-32 'He's already been named as king
and gone to Scone to be crowned.'

MACDUFF   He is already named, and gone to Scone
To be invested.

Scone = palace where
Scottish kings were crowned

ROSSE   Where is Duncan's body?

MACDUFF   Carried to Colmekill,
The sacred storehouse of his predecessors,
And guardian of their bones.

33 Colmekill is an island,
also called Iona, where
Scottish kings were buried.

ROSSE   Will you to Scone?   35

36 Macduff's home is in Fife.

MACDUFF   No, cousin, I'll to Fife.

ROSSE   Well, I will thither.

MACDUFF   Well, may you see things well done there — adieu!
Lest our old robes sit easier than our new!

ROSSE   Farewell, father.

40-41 'God bless you and everyone
else who will turn bad into good
and make enemies into friends.'

OLD MAN   God's benison go with you, and with those   40
That would make good of bad, and friends of foes!

Exeunt

benison = blessing

Act 2 — Revision Summary

These questions are about the whole of <u>Act Two</u>. The point of them is to check you really know what's going on, and you know the language and the characters in microscopic detail too — because that's what you need to write a decent essay. Oh, and being able to look the answer up is NOT the same as KNOWING the answer. That means you've got to answer these questions again and again until you can do it <u>without</u> looking back at the play.

1) In <u>Act 2, Scene 1</u> what present does Banquo say Duncan has given to Lady Macbeth?

2) In lines 12-22 Banquo says,
"I dreamt last night of the weïrd sisters —
To you they have showed some truth."
Write at least two sentences to explain what Banquo means by "to you they have showed some truth".

3) Write Banquo's speech at lines 27-30 out again <u>in your own words</u>.

4) Is there anyone else on stage when Macbeth makes the "Is this a dagger which I see before me" speech?

5) Write down three phrases from lines 37-39 which describe the dagger as an illusion.

6) When Macbeth says "I see thee still" is he talking about the imaginary dagger or his real dagger?

7) What is the "bloody business" that Macbeth is talking about in line 49?

8) In the same speech, what exact words does Macbeth use to say "It's night"?

9) What does Macbeth do immediately after Act 2, Scene 1, and before Act 2, Scene 2?

10) At the beginning of <u>Act 2, Scene 2</u>, Lady Macbeth describes how she got Duncan's servants out of the way so Macbeth could murder Duncan. Did she:
a) get them drunk,   b) give them something to make them fall asleep,   c) both?

11) Why didn't Lady Macbeth kill Duncan herself?

12) What happened as Macbeth was coming downstairs to see Lady Macbeth?

13) What does "incarnadine" mean?

14) Would you describe the mood of Macbeth and Lady Macbeth in this scene as:
a) tranquil and serene,   b) joyful and affectionate,   or   c) tense and nervy?

15) Write down three phrases or sentences from Act 2, Scene 2, that show that Macbeth is feeling guilty.

16) Write down three phrases or sentences from the scene that show how Lady Macbeth feels about the murder. Then sum up her attitude in one sentence.

17) In <u>Act 2, Scene 3</u>, what three things does the porter say drinking "provokes"?

18) Why has Macduff come to the castle so early?

19) Quote <u>three</u> phrases that Macduff uses to describe what a stormy night it's been.

20) What's Macduff talking about when he says "O horror, horror, horror..." at line 56?

21) Quote three phrases or sentences that Macbeth or Lady Macbeth use to give the impression that they're surprised about the murder.

22) Who asks Macbeth why he killed the servants?

23) What are Duncan's sons called? Where does each one decide to go?

24) In <u>Act 2, Scene 4</u>, is it day or night? What does it look like?

25) What do Rosse and the Old Man say Duncan's horses did in the night?

26) Between line 22 and line 27, Rosse and Macduff discuss who murdered Duncan. Who do they say committed the murder? Who do they say planned the murder?

27) Who's going to be king now?

28) Where is he being crowned?

29) Rosse says he's going to the coronation. Is Macduff going with him?

Banquo suspects Macbeth of killing Duncan. Macbeth enters and flatters Banquo a bit, then finds out what he'll be doing that afternoon. Banquo leaves and Macbeth has a big moan about him. He orders two murderers to kill him and Fleance.

ACT 3 SCENE 1
The royal palace at Forres.

Enter BANQUO

1-3 'You've got it all now, Macbeth — king, Thane of Cawdor <u>and</u> Glamis — just as the witches promised, but I'm worried you've done something terrible to get it.'

stand in thy prosperity = stay in your family

BANQUO Thou hast it now — King, Cawdor, Glamis, all,
As the weird women promised, and, I fear,
Thou play'dst most foully for't. Yet it was said
It should not stand in thy posterity,
But that myself should be the root and father   5
Of many kings. If there come truth from them —
As upon thee, Macbeth, their speeches shine —
Why, by the verities on thee made good,
May they not be my oracles as well,
And set me up in hope? But hush! No more.   10

3-10 Banquo feels better, remembering that the Witches said he'd be the father of many kings. If what they said came true for Macbeth, then surely it will for him too.

sennet = trumpet fanfare

Sennet **sounded.** *Enter* MACBETH, *as king,* LADY MACBETH, *as queen,* LENNOX, ROSS, *Lords, Ladies, and Attendants.*

Banquo has been talking to himself. Now Macbeth and some others enter.

MACBETH Here's our chief guest.

11-15 Macbeth and Lady Macbeth suck up to Banquo.

LADY MACBETH   If he had been forgotten,
It had been as a gap in our great feast,
And all-thing unbecoming.

MACBETH To-night we hold a solemn supper sir,
And I'll request your presence.

indissoluble = unbreakable

BANQUO   Let your highness   15
Command upon me, to the which my duties
Are with a most indissoluble tie
For ever knit.

19,23,35 Macbeth is sneakily finding out what Banquo will be doing later on.

MACBETH Ride you this afternoon?

BANQUO   Ay, my good lord.

MACBETH We should have else desired your good advice,   20
Which still hath been both grave and prosperous,
In this day's council, but we'll take to-morrow.
Is't far you ride?

24-25 'I'll ride as far as I can between now and supper.'

BANQUO As far, my lord, as will fill up the time
'Twixt this and supper. Go not my horse the better,   25
I must become a borrower of the night
For a dark hour or twain.

27 'Don't miss our feast.'

MACBETH   Fail not our feast.

BANQUO My lord, I will not.

our bloody cousins = Malcolm and Donalbain

MACBETH We hear, our bloody cousins are bestowed
In England and in Ireland, not confessing   30
Their cruel parricide, filling their hearers
With strange invention — but of that to-morrow,
When therewithal we shall have cause of state
Craving us jointly. Hie you to horse. Adieu,
Till you return at night. Goes Fleance with you?   35

29-32 'Malcolm and Donalbain have gone to England and Ireland, without confessing to their Dad's murder, and telling all kinds of awful lies — but we'll talk about that tomorrow.'

BANQUO Ay, my good lord, our time does call upon 's.

MACBETH I wish your horses swift and sure of foot,
And so I do commend you to their backs. Farewell.

Exit BANQUO

39-42 'Everyone occupy yourselves until 7pm.'

Let every man be master of his time
Till seven at night. To make society   40

The sweeter welcome,
We will keep ourself till supper-time alone —
While then, God be with you!

Exeunt all but MACBETH, *and a* SERVANT
Sirrah, a word with you.
Attend those men our pleasure?

SERVANT They are, my lord,
Without the palace gate.

MACBETH Bring them before us. 45

Exit SERVANT
To be thus is nothing but to be safely thus.
Our fears in Banquo
Stick deep, and in his royalty of nature
Reigns that which would be feared. 'Tis much he dares,
And, to that dauntless temper of his mind, 50
He hath a wisdom that doth guide his valour
To act in safety. There is none but he
Whose being I do fear, and, under him,
My Genius is rebuked; as, it is said,
Mark Antony's was by Caesar. He chid the sisters 55
When first they put the name of king upon me,
And bade them speak to him. Then prophet-like
They hailed him father to a line of kings —
Upon my head they placed a fruitless crown,
And put a barren sceptre in my gripe, 60
Thence to be wrenched with an unlineal hand,
No son of mine succeeding. If 't be so,
For Banquo's issue have I filed my mind,
For them the gracious Duncan have I murdered;
Put rancours in the vessel of my peace 65
Only for them, and mine eternal jewel
Given to the common enemy of man,
To make them kings, the seed of Banquo kings!
Rather than so, come fate into the list,
And champion me to the utterance! Who's there? 70

Re-enter SERVANT, *with two* MURDERERS
Now go to the door, and stay there till we call.

Exit SERVANT
Was it not yesterday we spoke together?

FIRST MURDERER It was, so please your highness.

MACBETH Well then, now
Have you considered of my speeches? Know
That it was he in the times past which held you 75
So under fortune, which you thought had been
Our innocent self — this I made good to you
In our last conference, passed in probation with you,
How you were borne in hand, how crossed, the instruments,
Who wrought with them, and all things else that might 80
To half a soul and to a notion crazed
Say 'Thus did Banquo.'

FIRST MURDERER You made it known to us.

44 'Are those men here to see me?'

without = outside

46 'Just being King in name isn't enough — I need to feel secure in my position.'
47-53 Macbeth is worried about Banquo — he is a brave and wise man and the only man that Macbeth is afraid of.

Genius = guardian angel
54-55 In Ancient Rome, Mark Anthony and Octavius Caesar both wanted to be ruler, and Caesar won in the end.
55-58 'Banquo didn't like it when the witches said I'd be king and he asked them to speak to him too. Then they said he'd be father of many kings.'
59-68 'Having the crown is pointless if my sons don't succeed me. If it's true, then I've done this dreadful thing and murdered Duncan for the sake of Banquo's kids. I've turned peace to hostility and have given my soul to the devil — all for them!'
issue = children
eternal jewel = soul
69-70 Macbeth thinks this is so bad that he wants to challenge fate to a fight to the death.
list = jousting arena

74-82 When Macbeth spoke to the murderers the day before, he told them that Banquo is their enemy.
passed in probation = looked over the proof
bad... good...

83-90 *Macbeth taunts the murderers, saying they're not man enough to take revenge on Banquo. 'Are you such wimps that you're going to let him get away with this?'*

gospelled = religious

MACBETH   I did so, and went further, which is now
Our point of second meeting. Do you find
Your patience so predominant in your nature   85
That you can let this go? Are you so gospelled
To pray for this good man and for his issue,
Whose heavy hand hath bowed you to the grave
And beggared yours for ever?

89 *'Oi, we're not wimps, we're men!'*

FIRST MURDERER   We are men, my liege.

90-106 *'You say you're men but, like dogs, there are lots of different types of man, each with different qualities. If you are high quality men then say it, and I'll help you to kill your enemy.'*

clept = called

MACBETH   Ay, in the catalogue ye go for men,   90
As hounds and greyhounds, mongrels, spaniels, curs,
Shoughs, water-rugs and demi-wolves, are clept
All by the name of dogs. The valued file
Distinguishes the swift, the slow, the subtle,
The housekeeper, the hunter, every one   95
According to the gift which bounteous nature
Hath in him closed, whereby he does receive
Particular addition, from the bill
That writes them all alike — and so of men.
Now, if you have a station in the file,   100
Not i' the worst rank of manhood, say 't,
And I will put that business in your bosoms,
Whose execution takes your enemy off,

104 *'You'll have my affection and gratitude.'*

Grapples you to the heart and love of us,
Who wear our health but sickly in his life,   105
Which in his death were perfect.

106-109 *'I've had such a horrible life that I'll do anything to get back at the world.'*

SECOND MURDERER   I am one, my liege,
Whom the vile blows and buffets of the world
Have so incensed that I am reckless what
I do to spite the world.

109-112 *'Same here.'*

FIRST MURDERER   And I another
So weary with disasters, tugged with fortune,   110
That I would set my lie on any chance,
To mend it, or be rid on't.

MACBETH   Both of you
Know Banquo was your enemy.

BOTH MURDERERS.   True, my lord.

114-124 *'Banquo is my enemy too — and such a bad one that he threatens my existence. I could just use my power to get rid of him openly but I won't, because we have mutual friends who I don't want to upset. So I'm getting you to help me, to keep his murder out of the public eye.'*

MACBETH   So is he mine; and in such bloody distance,
That every minute of his being thrusts   115
Against my near'st of life — and though I could
With barefaced power sweep him from my sight
And bid my will avouch it, yet I must not,
For certain friends that are both his and mine,
Whose loves I may not drop, but wail his fall   120
Who I myself struck down; and thence it is,
That I to your assistance do make love,
Masking the business from the common eye
For sundry weighty reasons.

SECOND MURDERER   We shall, my lord,
Perform what you command us.

FIRST MURDERER   Though our lives —   125

126-130 *Macbeth interrupts the first Murderer, to give them the details about when and where to do the dirty deed.*

perfect spy o' the time = the exact time

MACBETH   Your spirits shine through you. Within this hour at most
I will advise you where to plant yourselves.
Acquaint you with the perfect spy o' the time,

The moment on't, for't must be done to-night,
And something from the palace, always thought   130
That I require a clearness — and with him
To leave no rubs nor botches in the work —
Fleance his son, that keeps him company,
Whose absence is no less material to me
Than is his father's, must embrace the fate   135
Of that dark hour. Resolve yourselves apart —
I'll come to you anon.

BOTH MURDERERS   We are resolved, my lord.

MACBETH I'll call upon you straight. Abide within.

Exeunt MURDERERS
It is concluded. Banquo, thy soul's flight,
If it find heaven, must find it out to-night.   140

Exit

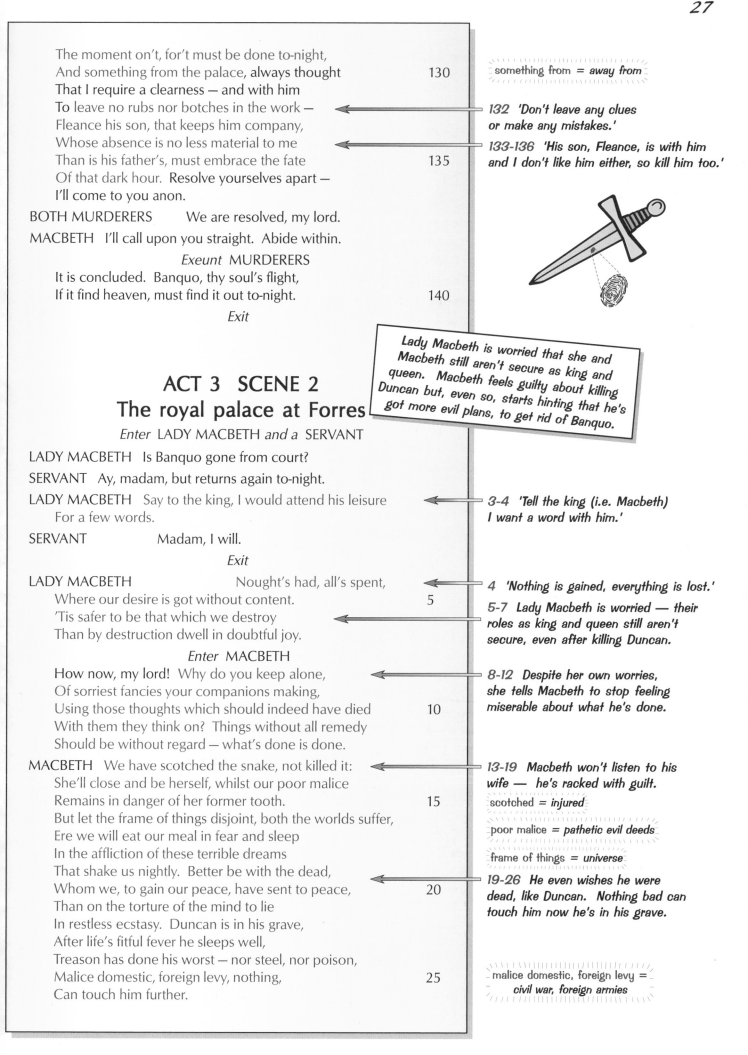

something from = away from

132 'Don't leave any clues or make any mistakes.'

133-136 'His son, Fleance, is with him and I don't like him either, so kill him too.'

ACT 3 SCENE 2
The royal palace at Forres

Lady Macbeth is worried that she and Macbeth still aren't secure as king and queen. Macbeth feels guilty about killing Duncan but, even so, starts hinting that he's got more evil plans, to get rid of Banquo.

Enter LADY MACBETH *and a* SERVANT

LADY MACBETH Is Banquo gone from court?

SERVANT Ay, madam, but returns again to-night.

LADY MACBETH Say to the king, I would attend his leisure
For a few words.

3-4 'Tell the king (i.e. Macbeth) I want a word with him.'

SERVANT   Madam, I will.

Exit

LADY MACBETH   Nought's had, all's spent,
Where our desire is got without content.   5
'Tis safer to be that which we destroy
Than by destruction dwell in doubtful joy.

4 'Nothing is gained, everything is lost.'

5-7 Lady Macbeth is worried — their roles as king and queen still aren't secure, even after killing Duncan.

Enter MACBETH
How now, my lord! Why do you keep alone,
Of sorriest fancies your companions making,
Using those thoughts which should indeed have died 10
With them they think on? Things without all remedy
Should be without regard — what's done is done.

8-12 Despite her own worries, she tells Macbeth to stop feeling miserable about what he's done.

MACBETH We have scotched the snake, not killed it:
She'll close and be herself, whilst our poor malice
Remains in danger of her former tooth.   15
But let the frame of things disjoint, both the worlds suffer,
Ere we will eat our meal in fear and sleep
In the affliction of these terrible dreams
That shake us nightly. Better be with the dead,
Whom we, to gain our peace, have sent to peace,   20
Than on the torture of the mind to lie
In restless ecstasy. Duncan is in his grave,
After life's fitful fever he sleeps well,
Treason has done his worst — nor steel, nor poison,
Malice domestic, foreign levy, nothing,   25
Can touch him further.

13-19 Macbeth won't listen to his wife — he's racked with guilt.
scotched = injured
poor malice = pathetic evil deeds
frame of things = universe

19-26 He even wishes he were dead, like Duncan. Nothing bad can touch him now he's in his grave.

malice domestic, foreign levy = civil war, foreign armies

28

26-28 'Calm down and make yourself presentable. Be jolly for your guests tonight.'

30-31 'Be extra nice to Banquo tonight — pay him lots of attention.'

32-35 'We're not safe yet. We must keep up this flattery to disguise what we're really thinking.'

lave = wash

vizards = masks

38 'But they won't live forever.'

39-44 'Don't worry — we'll get them. Before the night is done, something bad is going to happen.'

assailable = able to be attacked

jocund = merry

Hecate = goddess of witches

shard-borne = flying

45-46 'I'm not telling you what it is until it's all done and dusted.'

46-53 Macbeth wants night to come quickly so the dark deeds can begin.

seeling = blinding

LADY MACBETH   Come on,
Gentle my lord, sleek o'er your rugged looks.
Be bright and jovial among your guests to-night.

MACBETH   So shall I, love, and so, I pray, be you —
Let your remembrance apply to Banquo;   30
Present him eminence, both with eye and tongue:
Unsafe the while, that we
Must lave our honours in these flattering streams,
And make our faces vizards to our hearts,
Disguising what they are.

LADY MACBETH   You must leave this.   35

MACBETH   O, full of scorpions is my mind, dear wife!
Thou know'st that Banquo, and his Fleance, lives.

LADY MACBETH   But in them nature's copy's not eterne.

MACBETH   There's comfort yet. They are assailable,
Then be thou jocund — ere the bat hath flown   40
His cloister'd flight, ere to black Hecate's summons
The shard-borne beetle with his drowsy hums
Hath rung night's yawning peal, there shall be done
A deed of dreadful note.

LADY MACBETH   What's to be done?

MACBETH   Be innocent of the knowledge, dearest chuck, 45
Till thou applaud the deed. Come, seeling night,
Scarf up the tender eye of pitiful day,
And with thy bloody and invisible hand
Cancel and tear to pieces that great bond
Which keeps me pale! Light thickens, and the crow   50
Makes wing to the rooky wood.
Good things of day begin to droop and drowse,
While night's black agents to their preys do rouse.
Thou marvell'st at my words — but hold thee still,
Things bad begun make strong themselves by ill.   55
So, prithee, go with me.

Exeunt

Macbeth has sent another murderer to join the first two. As Banquo and Fleance approach the palace, they manage to kill Banquo, but Fleance escapes.

ACT 3 SCENE 3
Park near the palace
Enter three MURDERERS.

FIRST MURDERER   But who did bid thee join with us?

THIRD MURDERER   Macbeth.

SECOND MURDERER   He needs not our mistrust, since he delivers
Our offices and what we have to do
To the direction just.

FIRST MURDERER   Then stand with us.
The west yet glimmers with some streaks of day   5
Now spurs the lated traveller apace
To gain the timely inn, and near approaches
The subject of our watch.

THIRD MURDERER   Hark! I hear horses.

2-3 'We can trust him, because he's told us exactly what we have to do.'

offices = duties

5 Sunset is nearly over.

the subject of our watch = Banquo and Fleance

BANQUO *(Within)* Give us a light there, ho!

SECOND MURDERER   Then 'tis he — the rest
    That are within the note of expectation   10
    Already are i' the court.

9-11 'It's him — everyone else who's expected for dinner is already there.'

FIRST MURDERER   His horses go about.

go about = turn back

THIRD MURDERER   Almost a mile — but he does usually,
    So all men do, from hence to the palace gate
    Make it their walk.

13-14 He says people normally walk the last mile to the palace gate.

SECOND MURDERER   A light, a light!

           Enter BANQUO, *and* FLEANCE *with a torch.*

THIRD MURDERER   'Tis he.

FIRST MURDERER   Stand to't.   15

BANQUO   It will be rain to-night.

FIRST MURDERER   Let it come down.

            They set upon BANQUO.

BANQUO   O, treachery! Fly, good Fleance, fly, fly, fly!
    Thou mayst revenge. O slave!

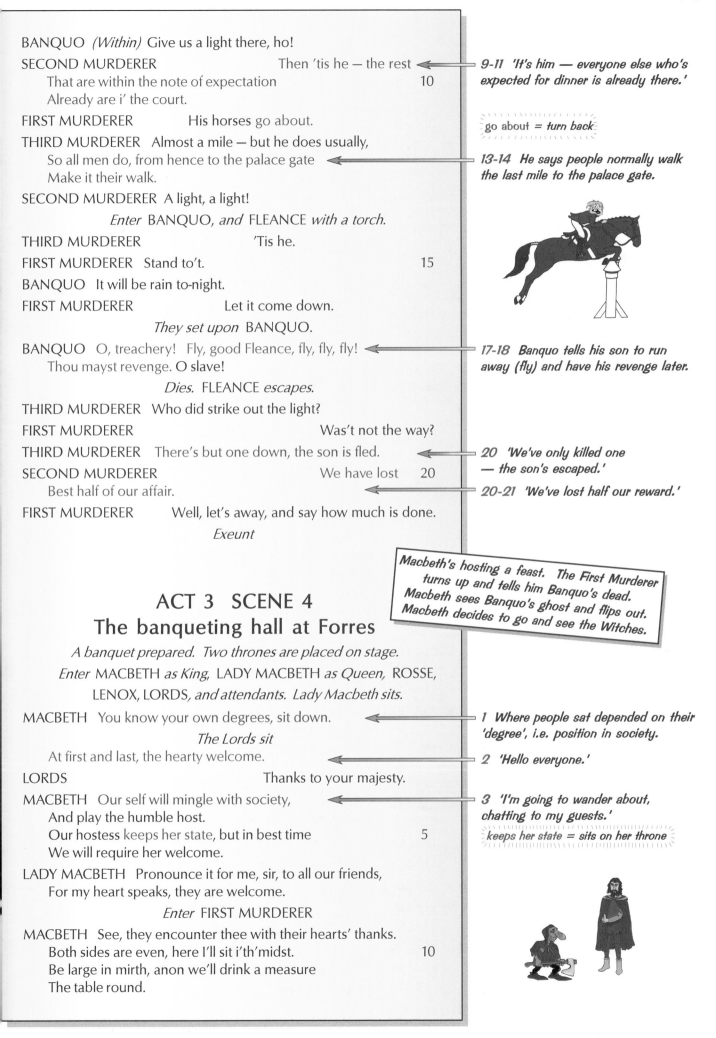

17-18 Banquo tells his son to run away (fly) and have his revenge later.

          Dies. FLEANCE *escapes.*

THIRD MURDERER   Who did strike out the light?

FIRST MURDERER   Was't not the way?

THIRD MURDERER   There's but one down, the son is fled.

20 'We've only killed one — the son's escaped.'

SECOND MURDERER   We have lost   20
    Best half of our affair.

20-21 'We've lost half our reward.'

FIRST MURDERER   Well, let's away, and say how much is done.

                Exeunt

ACT 3 SCENE 4
The banqueting hall at Forres

A banquet prepared. Two thrones are placed on stage.
Enter MACBETH *as King,* LADY MACBETH *as Queen,* ROSSE,
LENOX, LORDS, *and attendants. Lady Macbeth sits.*

Macbeth's hosting a feast. The First Murderer turns up and tells him Banquo's dead. Macbeth sees Banquo's ghost and flips out. Macbeth decides to go and see the Witches.

MACBETH   You know your own degrees, sit down.

1 Where people sat depended on their 'degree', i.e. position in society.

              The Lords sit
    At first and last, the hearty welcome.

2 'Hello everyone.'

LORDS   Thanks to your majesty.

MACBETH   Our self will mingle with society,
    And play the humble host.
    Our hostess keeps her state, but in best time   5
    We will require her welcome.

3 'I'm going to wander about, chatting to my guests.'

keeps her state = sits on her throne

LADY MACBETH   Pronounce it for me, sir, to all our friends,
    For my heart speaks, they are welcome.

            Enter FIRST MURDERER

MACBETH   See, they encounter thee with their hearts' thanks.
    Both sides are even, here I'll sit i'th'midst.   10
    Be large in mirth, anon we'll drink a measure
    The table round.

14-15 *'I'd rather see his blood on your face than in him. Is he dead?'*

17-19 *'You're a good killer. Whoever killed Fleance is good, too. If you did that too, you're the best.'*

scaped = escaped

21-25 *'I'd have been completely safe if you'd killed Fleance as well, but now I'm trapped by worry.'*

safe = safely done away with

29-31 *He means Banquo's dead, and his young son will be a problem when he's older, but not yet.*

37 *'Thanks for reminding me.'*
38-39 *'Tuck in.'*

40-41 *'We'd be in the most honoured place in the country if Banquo was here.'*

42-43 *'I hope I get to tell him off for not being here, rather than pity him for being in an accident.' Pretty evil given Macbeth's just had him killed.*

43-44 *'He said he'd be here, so he should have made sure he was.'*

48 *'What's bugging you?'*

(To First Murderer) There's blood upon thy face.

FIRST MURDERER   'Tis Banquo's then.

MACBETH   'Tis better thee without, than he within.
Is he dispatched?   15

FIRST MURDERER   My lord, his throat is cut, that I did for him.

MACBETH   Thou art the best o'th'cut-throats,
Yet he's good that did the like for Fleance;
If thou didst it, thou art the nonpareil.

FIRST MURDERER   Most royal sir, Fleance is scaped.   20

MACBETH   Then comes my fit again — I had else been perfect;
Whole as the marble, founded as the rock,
As broad and general as the casing air.
But now I am cabined, cribbed, confined, bound in
To saucy doubts and fears. But Banquo's safe?   25

FIRST MURDERER   Ay, my good lord, safe in a ditch he bides,
With twenty trenched gashes on his head,
The least a death to nature.

MACBETH   Thanks for that.
There the grown serpent lies, the worm that's fled
Hath nature that in time will venom breed,   30
No teeth for th'present. Get thee gone. Tomorrow
We'll hear ourselves again.

Exit FIRST MURDERER

LADY MACBETH   My royal lord,
You do not give the cheer, the feast is sold
That is not often vouched while 'tis a-making
'Tis given with welcome. To feed were best at home. 35
From thence, the sauce to meat is ceremony,
Meeting were bare without it.

Enter the GHOST OF BANQUO
and sits in Macbeth's place

MACBETH   Sweet remembrancer!
Now good digestion wait on appetite,
And health on both.

LENOX   May't please your highness, sit.

MACBETH   Here had we now our country's honour roofed,   40
Were the graced person of our Banquo present,
Who may I rather challenge for unkindness
Than pity for mischance.

ROSSE   His absence, sir,
Lays blame upon his promise. Please't your highness
To grace us with your royal company?   45

MACBETH   The table's full.

LENOX   Here is a place reserved, sir.

MACBETH   Where?

LENOX   Here, my good lord. What is't that moves your highness?

MACBETH   Which of you have done this?

LORDS   What, my good lord?

MACBETH   Thou canst not say I did it; never shake   50
Thy gory locks at me!

ROSSE   Gentlemen, rise, his highness is not well.

LADY MACBETH joins the Lords.

LADY MACBETH   Sit, worthy friends. My lord is often thus,
   And hath been from his youth. Pray you, keep seat.
   The fit is momentary. Upon a thought   55
   He will again be well. If much you note him
   You shall offend him and extend his passion.
   Feed, and regard him not. (*To Macbeth*) Are you a man?

MACBETH   Ay, and a bold one, that dare look on that
   Which might appal the devil.

LADY MACBETH   O proper stuff!   60
   This is the very painting of your fear,
   This is the air-drawn dagger which you said
   Led you to Duncan. O, these flaws and starts,
   Impostors to true fear, would well become
   A woman's story at a winter's fire   65
   Authorised by her grandam. Shame itself!
   Why do you make such faces? When all's done
   You look but on a stool.

MACBETH   Prithee, see there! Behold, look, lo! How say you?
   (*To Ghost*) Why, what care I? If thou canst nod, speak too. 70
   If charnel houses and our graves must send
   Those that we bury back, our monuments
   Shall be the maws of kites.

Exit GHOST OF BANQUO

LADY MACBETH   What, quite unmanned in folly?

MACBETH   If I stand here, I saw him.

LADY MACBETH   Fie, for shame.

MACBETH   Blood hath been shed ere now, i'th'olden time,   75
   Ere humane statute purged the gentle weal.
   Ay, and since too, murders have been performed
   Too terrible for the ear. The time has been
   That when the brains were out, the man would die,
   And there an end. But now they rise again   80
   With twenty mortal murders on their crowns
   And push us from our stools. This is more strange
   Than such a murder is.

LADY MACBETH   My worthy lord,
   Your noble friends do lack you.

MACBETH   I do forget —
   Do not muse at me, my most worthy friends.   85
   I have a strange infirmity which is nothing
   To those that know me. Come, love and health to all,
   Then I'll sit down. Give me some wine, fill full!

Enter GHOST OF BANQUO

   I drink to th'general joy o'th'whole table,
   And to our dear friend Banquo, whom we miss.   90
   Would he were here! To all, and him, we thirst,
   And all to all.

LORDS   Our duties and the pledge.

MACBETH   Avaunt and quit my sight! Let the earth hide thee!

keep seat = stay sat down.

55-57 'He'll be OK in a minute, but he'll get worse if you make a fuss.'

58 'Don't pay him any attention.'

60-68 'Rubbish. You're seeing things. It's just a chair.'

...then the witches and I had a really lovely bit of fruit cake, very moist...

69 'But look, it's there.'

71-73 'If, when you put a body into a grave, it comes back, we'll have to feed bodies to the birds of prey so they can't come back.'

kite = bird of prey

73 'So upset by nothing?'

75-80 'There have been murders in the past, but it used to be that when you killed people, they stayed dead. Not any more.'

84 'Don't forget to talk to the Thanes.'

85-87 'Don't worry, I have an illness that makes me go like this, but it's not really a problem.'

91 'I wish Banquo was here.'

93 'Get out of here!'

Act 3, Scene 4

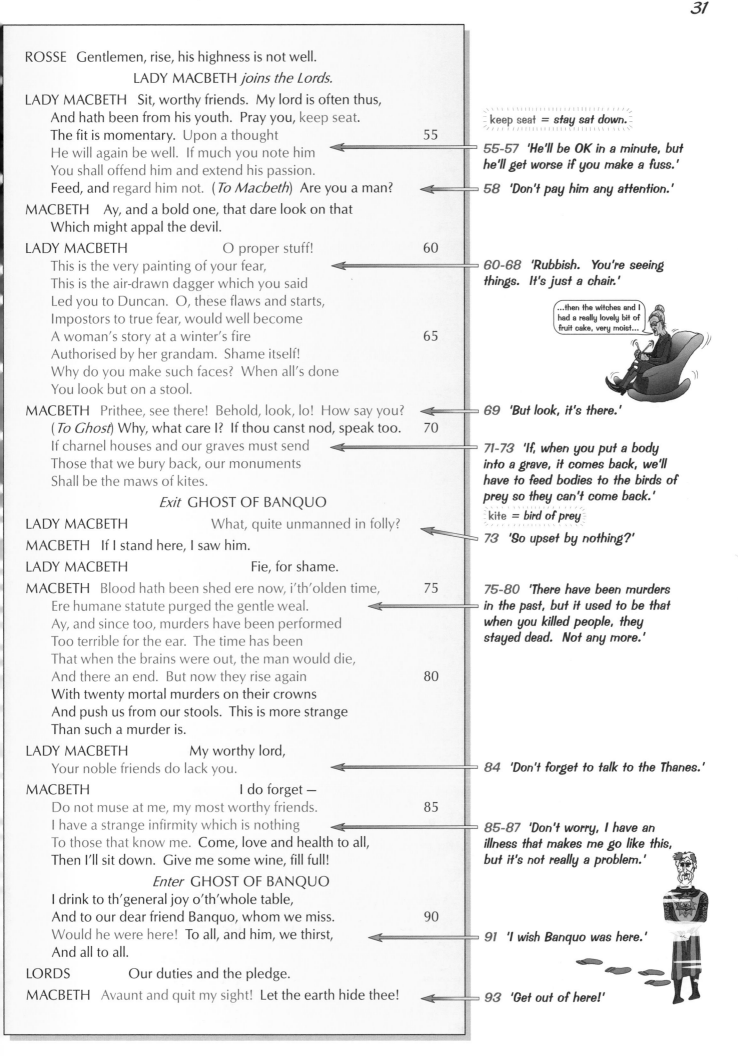

32

speculation = sight

Thy bones are marrowless, thy blood is cold;
Thou hast no speculation in those eyes   95
Which thou dost glare with.

96-97 'He's often like this.'

LADY MACBETH   Think of this, good peers,
But as a thing of custom. 'Tis no other,
Only it spoils the pleasure of the time.

99-106 'I'm as brave as any man. There's nothing else I'd be scared of — if I was, you could call me a baby girl.'

MACBETH   What man dare, I dare.
Approach thou like the rugged Russian bear,   100
The armed rhinoceros, or th'Hyrcan tiger.
Take any shape but that, and my firm nerves
Shall never tremble. Or be alive again,
And dare me to the desert with thy sword —
If trembling I inhabit then, protest me   105
The baby of a girl. Hence horrible shadow!
Unreal mockery, hence!

Exit GHOST OF BANQUO
                    Why so, being gone,
I am a man again. Pray you, sit still.

109-110 'You've ruined the feast by being so weird.'

LADY MACBETH   You have displaced the mirth, broke the good
                                                        meeting
With most admired disorder.

110-116 'Of course I'm in a state, anyone would be. You make me feel I'm not the brave person I thought I was, since you aren't scared to see a ghost.'

MACBETH   Can such things be,   110
And overcome us like a summer's cloud,
Without our special wonder? You make me strange
Even to the disposition that I owe,
When now I think you can behold such sights
And keep the natural ruby of your cheeks,   115
When mine is blanched with fear.

ROSSE   What sights, my lord?

117-118 'Don't ask him. Questions will make him even worse. Everyone go at once.'

LADY MACBETH   I pray you speak not, he grows worse and worse.
Question enrages him. At once, good night.
Stand not upon the order of your going,
But go at once.

119-120 People would normally leave in order of importance, but Lady Macbeth tells them all to just go straight away.

LENOX   Good night, and better health   120
Attend his majesty.

LADY MACBETH   A kind good night to all.

Exeunt LORDS *and Attendants*

MACBETH   It will have blood they say — blood will have blood.
Stones have been known to move and trees to speak.
Augures, and understood relations, have
By maggot-pies, and choughs, and rooks brought forth   125

maggot-pies = magpies
choughs = birds a bit like crows

126 'What time is it?'

The secret'st man of blood. What is the night?

127 'Almost morning.'

LADY MACBETH   Almost at odds with morning, which is which.

128-129 'How come Macduff hasn't come?'

MACBETH   How sayst thou that Macduff denies his person
At our great bidding?

LADY MACBETH   Did you send to him, sir?

MACBETH   I hear it by the way, but I will send.   130

131-132 'I pay a servant to be my spy in every one of the Thanes' houses.'

There's not a one of them but in his house
I keep a servant fee'd. I will tomorrow —

132-133 'Tomorrow I'm going off early to see the three Witches.'

And betimes I will — to the weïrd sisters.

More shall they speak. For now I am bent to know
By the worst means, the worst.   For mine own good,   135
All causes shall give way. I am in blood
Stepped in so far that should I wade no more,
Returning were as tedious as go o'er.
Strange things I have in head that will to hand,
Which must be acted ere they may be scanned.   140

136-140 'I've killed so many people that it would be as hard to stop as to keep on killing. I've got things in mind that must be done before I think them over.'

LADY MACBETH   You lack the season of all natures, sleep.

MACBETH   Come, we'll to sleep. My strange and self-abuse
   Is the initiate fear that wants hard use.
   We are yet but young in deed.

142-143 'I'm being weird because I'm not used to acting tough.'

144 'We've still got to do a lot more.'

Exeunt

ACT 3   SCENE 5
A heath

Thunder. Enter the three Witches meeting HECATE.

Hecate is annoyed that the Witches spoke to Macbeth without involving her. She tells them to meet her at the pit of Acheron, to tell Macbeth his future. She is going to make an evil spell that will destroy Macbeth.

1ST WITCH   Why, how now, Hecate! You look angerly.

HECATE   Have I not reason, beldams as you are,
   Saucy and overbold? How did you dare
   To trade and traffic with Macbeth
   In riddles and affairs of death;   5
   And I, the mistress of your charms,
   The close contriver of all harms,
   Was never called to bear my part,
   Or show the glory of our art?
   And, which is worse, all you have done   10
   Hath been but for a wayward son,
   Spiteful and wrathful, who, as others do,
   Loves for his own ends, not for you.
   But make amends now — get you gone,
   And at the pit of Acheron   15
   Meet me i' the morning: thither he
   Will come to know his destiny —
   Your vessels and your spells provide,
   Your charms and every thing beside.
   I am for the air, this night I'll spend   20
   Unto a dismal and a fatal end.
   Great business must be wrought ere noon —
   Upon the corner of the moon
   There hangs a vaporous drop profound,
   I'll catch it ere it come to ground.   25
   And that distilled by magic sleights
   Shall raise such artificial sprites
   As by the strength of their illusion
   Shall draw him on to his confusion.
   He shall spurn fate, scorn death, and bear   30
   He hopes 'bove wisdom, grace and fear —
   And you all know, security
   Is mortals' chiefest enemy.

Hecate = goddess of witches

beldams = hags

3-9 'How dare you use your riddles on Macbeth without involving me, your mistress!'

10-13 'What's worse, you've done all this for nothing but a spiteful man who only cares about himself.'

14-17 'To make up for it, meet me at the pit of Acheron in the morning, where Macbeth will come to discover his destiny.

Acheron = a river in Hell

20-31 She's going to spend the night making a spell to create apparitions that will confuse Macbeth by making him over-confident, so that he thinks he can't die.

vaporous drop profound = magic potion

sleights = tricks

artificial sprites = apparitions

32-33 'And, as you all know, over-confidence is man's greatest enemy.

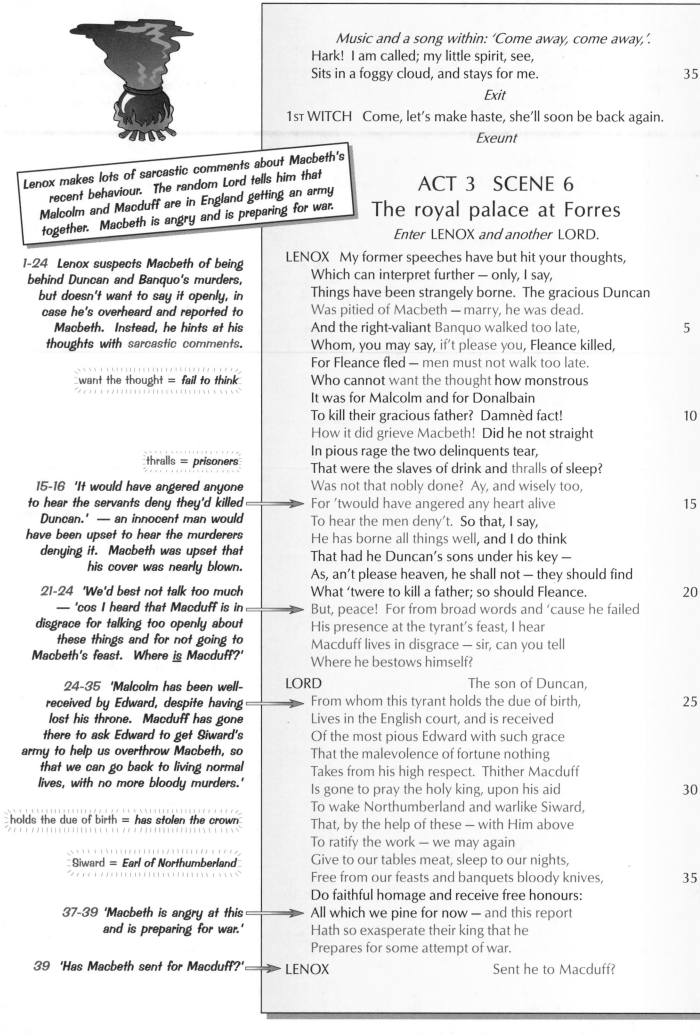

Lenox makes lots of sarcastic comments about Macbeth's recent behaviour. The random Lord tells him that Malcolm and Macduff are in England getting an army together. Macbeth is angry and is preparing for war.

Music and a song within: 'Come away, come away,'.
Hark! I am called; my little spirit, see,
Sits in a foggy cloud, and stays for me.   35

Exit

1ST WITCH   Come, let's make haste, she'll soon be back again.

Exeunt

ACT 3   SCENE 6
The royal palace at Forres

Enter LENOX and another LORD.

1-24 *Lenox suspects Macbeth of being behind Duncan and Banquo's murders, but doesn't want to say it openly, in case he's overheard and reported to Macbeth. Instead, he hints at his thoughts with sarcastic comments.*

want the thought = fail to think

thralls = prisoners

15-16 *'It would have angered anyone to hear the servants deny they'd killed Duncan.' — an innocent man would have been upset to hear the murderers denying it. Macbeth was upset that his cover was nearly blown.*

21-24 *'We'd best not talk too much — 'cos I heard that Macduff is in disgrace for talking too openly about these things and for not going to Macbeth's feast. Where is Macduff?'*

24-35 *'Malcolm has been well-received by Edward, despite having lost his throne. Macduff has gone there to ask Edward to get Siward's army to help us overthrow Macbeth, so that we can go back to living normal lives, with no more bloody murders.'*

holds the due of birth = has stolen the crown

Siward = Earl of Northumberland

37-39 *'Macbeth is angry at this and is preparing for war.'*

39 *'Has Macbeth sent for Macduff?'*

LENOX   My former speeches have but hit your thoughts,
Which can interpret further — only, I say,
Things have been strangely borne. The gracious Duncan
Was pitied of Macbeth — marry, he was dead.
And the right-valiant Banquo walked too late,   5
Whom, you may say, if't please you, Fleance killed,
For Fleance fled — men must not walk too late.
Who cannot want the thought how monstrous
It was for Malcolm and for Donalbain
To kill their gracious father? Damnèd fact!   10
How it did grieve Macbeth! Did he not straight
In pious rage the two delinquents tear,
That were the slaves of drink and thralls of sleep?
Was not that nobly done? Ay, and wisely too,
For 'twould have angered any heart alive   15
To hear the men deny't. So that, I say,
He has borne all things well, and I do think
That had he Duncan's sons under his key —
As, an't please heaven, he shall not — they should find
What 'twere to kill a father; so should Fleance.   20
But, peace! For from broad words and 'cause he failed
His presence at the tyrant's feast, I hear
Macduff lives in disgrace — sir, can you tell
Where he bestows himself?

LORD   The son of Duncan,
From whom this tyrant holds the due of birth,   25
Lives in the English court, and is received
Of the most pious Edward with such grace
That the malevolence of fortune nothing
Takes from his high respect. Thither Macduff
Is gone to pray the holy king, upon his aid   30
To wake Northumberland and warlike Siward,
That, by the help of these — with Him above
To ratify the work — we may again
Give to our tables meat, sleep to our nights,
Free from our feasts and banquets bloody knives,   35
Do faithful homage and receive free honours:
All which we pine for now — and this report
Hath so exasperate their king that he
Prepares for some attempt of war.

LENOX   Sent he to Macduff?

LORD   He did — and with an absolute 'Sir, not I,'   40
  The cloudy messenger turns me his back,
  And hums, as who should say 'You'll rue the time
  That clogs me with this answer.'
LENOX   And that well might
  Advise him to a caution, to hold what distance
  His wisdom can provide. Some holy angel   45
  Fly to the court of England and unfold
  His message ere he come, that a swift blessing
  May soon return to this our suffering country
  Under a hand accursed!
LORD   I'll send my prayers with him.
                    Exeunt

40-43 Macduff's message was, "Sir, not I", i.e. "No way am I coming back." The messenger is 'cloudy' because he doesn't want to be responsible for Macbeth getting this bad news.

cloudy = *sulky*

hums = *mutters*

Act 3 — Revision Summary

QUESTION: Which is more fun? a) wading through hundreds of lines of practically prehistoric, incredibly complicated poetry about a man going off his head in a remote castle in Scotland, b) answering an endless list of irritatingly picky questions, or c) an extra-large pepperoni pizza. ANSWER: c). Sadly this is a book, not a pizza restaurant. Just read Act 3 and answer the questions.

1) At the start of <u>Act 3, Scene 1</u> what are the exact words Banquo uses that show he knows Macbeth didn't just become king by accident?

2) What are the Macbeths planning for the evening?

3) What does Banquo say he's going to do until evening?

4) In Macbeth's long speech from line 46 to line 70 find short quotes that show:
a) Banquo's the only person Macbeth's afraid of,
b) Macbeth is angry that Banquo's descendants will be kings,
c) that Macbeth feels it may have been a mistake to kill Duncan.

5) What reason does Macbeth give for not having Banquo killed publicly?

6) What instructions does Macbeth give the Murderers about where and when they should kill Banquo?

7) Who else are the Murderers supposed to kill?

8) At the beginning of <u>Act 3, Scene 2</u> Lady Macbeth says she's not happy even though they've got what they wanted. Rewrite her speech from line 4 to line 7 <u>in your own words</u>.

9) Write a one-sentence summary of what Macbeth says in lines 13-26.

10) Does Macbeth actually tell Lady Macbeth he's planning to kill Banquo in this scene?

11) At line 36 Macbeth says "O, full of scorpions is my mind, dear wife!". Write down what he means in your own words.

12) In <u>Act 3, Scene 3</u> there are three Murderers. How many did Macbeth hire originally?

13) What time of day is it? Quote the exact words that tell you.

14) Who escapes from the Murderers?

15) By line 6 of <u>Act 3, Scene 4</u> Macbeth's described where everyone is around the room. Where are the Lords, Macbeth and Lady Macbeth?

16) Write a sentence in your own words, saying how Macbeth feels in lines 24-25.

17) In line 29 what does Macbeth compare Banquo to? What does he compare Fleance to?

18) Why does Macbeth say "The table's full," at line 46?

19) Lady Macbeth keeps making the same excuse for Macbeth's odd behaviour. Find one of the places where she makes the excuse and quote the exact words.

20) Can anybody apart from Macbeth see Banquo's ghost?

21) Which Lord didn't come to the feast?

22) What is Macbeth planning to do in the morning?

23) At the end of the scene Macbeth says there will have to be more wrongdoing — what are the exact words that tell you this?

24) In <u>Act 3, Scene 5</u> who is Hecate?

25) Where are the witches going to meet up with Macbeth?

26) What is Hecate going to do during the night?

27) Is Hecate planning to help Macbeth?

28) In <u>Act 3, Scene 6</u>, when Lenox says Duncan's murder "did grieve Macbeth" does he mean it?

29) What's the English king's name?

30) Is Macduff on Macbeth's side?

ACT 4 SCENE 1
A deserted place near Forres

Thunder. Enter the three WITCHES.

FIRST WITCH   Thrice the brindled cat hath mewed.

SECOND WITCH   Thrice and once the hedge-pig whined.

THIRD WITCH   Harpier cries, "Tis time, 'tis time."

brindled = striped

hedge-pig = hedgehog

3 'Harpier' is the name of the third witch's familiar.

FIRST WITCH   Round about the cauldron go,
   In the poisoned entrails throw.   5
   Toad, that under cold stone
   Days and nights has thirty-one
   Sweltered venom sleeping got,
   Boil thou first i'th' charmèd pot.

6-8 'a toad that has been under a stone sweating venom, for a month'

ALL   Double, double toil and trouble,   10
   Fire burn, and cauldron bubble.

SECOND WITCH   Fillet of a fenny snake,
   In the cauldron boil and bake.
   Eye of newt, and toe of frog,
   Wool of bat, and tongue of dog,   15
   Adder's fork, and blind-worm's sting,
   Lizard's leg, and howlet's wing,
   For a charm of powerful trouble,
   Like a hell-broth, boil and bubble.

12 'slice of a snake from the fens'

blind-worm = slow-worm (they're not poisonous really)

howlet = young owl

ALL Double, double toil and trouble,   20
   Fire burn, and cauldron bubble.

THIRD WITCH   Scale of dragon, tooth of wolf,
   Witches' mummy, maw and gulf
   Of the ravined salt-sea shark,
   Root of hemlock, digged i'th'dark,   25
   Liver of blaspheming Jew,
   Gall of goat, and slips of yew,
   Slivered in the moon's eclipse;
   Nose of Turk, and Tartar's lips,
   Finger of birth-strangled babe,   30
   Ditch-delivered by a drab,
   Make the gruel thick and slab.
   Add thereto a tiger's chawdron
   For th'ingredience of our cauldron.

23-24 'bits of mummified witch, the stomach and throat of a shark that's eaten its prey'

slips = cuttings

31 'born in a ditch with a prostitute as midwife'

slab = gooey

chawdron = intestines

ALL Double, double toil and trouble,   35
   Fire burn, and cauldron bubble.

SECOND WITCH   Cool it with a baboon's blood,
   Then the charm is firm and good.

Enter HECATE, *and three other Witches*

HECATE   O well done! I commend your pains,
   And every one shall share i'th'gains,   40
   And now about the cauldron sing
   Like elves and fairies in a ring,
   Enchanting all that you put in.

39-40 'Well done for putting the effort in. We'll all benefit from it.'

Music, and a song, 'Black spirits, etc.'

Exeunt Hecate and the three other Witches.

SECOND WITCH   By the pricking of my thumbs,

Something wicked this way comes. 45
Open locks, whoever knocks.

Enter MACBETH

MACBETH How now, you secret, black, and midnight hags!
What is't you do?

ALL THE WITCHES   A deed without a name.

MACBETH I conjure you by that which you profess,
However you come to know it, answer me. 50
Though you untie the winds and let them fight
Against the churches, though the yeasty waves
Confound and swallow navigation up,
Though bladed corn be lodged and trees blown down,
Though castles topple on their warders' heads, 55
Though palaces and pyramids do slope
Their heads to their foundations, though the treasure
Of nature's germen tumble altogether
Even till destruction sicken — answer me
To what I ask you.

FIRST WITCH   Speak.

SECOND WITCH   Demand.

THIRD WITCH   We'll answer, 60

FIRST WITCH Say, if thou'dst rather hear it from our mouths,
Or from our masters'?

MACBETH   Call 'em, let me see 'em.

FIRST WITCH Pour in sow's blood, that hath eaten
Her nine farrow; grease that's sweaten
From the murderer's gibbet throw 65
Into the flame.

ALL THE WITCHES Come high or low,
Thyself and office deftly show.

Thunder. Enter FIRST APPARITION, *an armed head.*

MACBETH Tell me, thou unknown power —

FIRST WITCH   He knows thy thought,
Hear his speech, but say thou nought.

FIRST APPARITION Macbeth! Macbeth! Macbeth! — beware
Macduff, 70
Beware the Thane of Fife. Dismiss me. Enough. *(Descends)*

MACBETH Whate'er thou art, for thy good caution, thanks.
Thou hast harped my fear aright. But one word more —

FIRST WITCH He will not be commanded. Here's another,
More potent than the first. 75

Thunder. Enter SECOND APPARITION, *a bloody child.*

SECOND APPARITION Macbeth! Macbeth! Macbeth!

MACBETH Had I three ears, I'd hear thee.

SECOND APPARITION Be bloody, bold, and resolute; laugh to scorn
The power of man, for none of woman born
Shall harm Macbeth. *(Descends)* 80

MACBETH Then live, Macduff, what need I fear of thee?
But yet I'll make assurance double sure.

Act 4, Scene 1

Side notes:

51-60 'Even if it means the destruction of everything, answer me.'

yeasty = frothy

confound and swallow navigation up = wreck ships

lodged = flattened

germen = cells

63-66 'Pour in the blood of a mother pig that's eaten her nine babies, and the sweat of a hanged murderer.'

67 'Show yourself and do your job.'

armed head = head in a helmet

68-69 'He knows what you're thinking — so just shut up and listen.'

Thane of Fife = Macduff

72-73 'Whatever you are, thanks for your good advice, I was already worried about that.'

potent = powerful

78-80 'Don't be afraid of anyone — no man born from a woman can hurt you.'

81-83 'Then it doesn't matter if Macduff lives — I don't have to be scared of him. But I'll make double sure and kill him.'

And take a bond of fate — thou shall not live,
That I may tell pale-hearted fear it lies,
And sleep in spite of thunder.

Thunder. Enter THIRD APPARITION,
a child crowned, with a tree in his hand.

What is this,   85
That rises like the issue of a king
And wears upon his baby brow the round
And top of sovereignty?

ALL THE WITCHES   Listen, but speak not to't.

THIRD APPARITION   Be lion-mettled, proud, and take no care
Who chafes, who frets, or where conspirers are.   90
Macbeth shall never vanquished be until
Great Birnam wood to high Dunsinane hill
Shall come against him. *(Descends)*

MACBETH   That will never be:
Who can impress the forest, bid the tree
Unfix his earthbound root? Sweet bodements, good.   95
Rebellious dead, rise never till the wood
Of Birnam rise, and our high-placed Macbeth
Shall live the lease of nature, pay his breath
To time and mortal custom. Yet my heart
Throbs to know one thing. Tell me, if your art   100
Can tell so much, shall Banquo's issue ever
Reign in this kingdom?

ALL THE WITCHES   Seek to know no more.

MACBETH   I will be satisfied. Deny me this,
And an eternal curse fall on you. Let me know.

Cauldron descends. Hautboys.
Why sinks that cauldron? And what noise is this?   105

FIRST WITCH   Show!

SECOND WITCH   Show!

THIRD WITCH   Show!

ALL THE WITCHES   Show his eyes and grieve his heart,
Come like shadows, so depart,   110

*Enter a show of eight kings, and the last with a
glass in his hand,* BANQUO'S GHOST *following*

MACBETH   Thou art too like the spirit of Banquo. Down!
Thy crown does sear mine eyeballs. And thy hair,
Thou other gold-bound brow, is like the first;
A third, is like the former. — Filthy hags,
Why do you show me this? — A fourth? Start, eyes!   115
What, will the line stretch out to th'crack of doom?
Another yet? A seventh? I'll see no more.
And yet the eighth appears, who bears a glass
Which shows me many more. And some I see,
That two-fold balls and treble sceptres carry.   120
Horrible sight! Now I see 'tis true,
For the blood-boltered Banquo smiles upon me,
And points at them for his.

Exeunt show of kings and BANQUO'S GHOST

issue = *child*

the round and top of sovereignty = *the crown*

89-93 *'Be brave, and don't be bothered by people complaining or conspiring against you, because you won't be beaten until Birnam wood moves to Dunsinane hill.'*

93-95 *'That'll never happen — no-one can tell a forest to move.'*

99-102 *'I'm desperate to know, if you can tell me, whether Banquo's descendants will ever be kings?'*

hautboys = *musical instrument, like an oboe*

glass = *mirror*

111-123 *Macbeth isn't too chuffed to see so many people who look like Banquo, all wearing crowns.*

116 *'Will the line go on for ever?'*

119-120 *'I can see some carrying two orbs and three sceptres.'* Banquo's descendants are going to end up ruling England as well as Scotland.

blood-boltered = *matted with blood*

123 *Banquo's ghost is pointing to show that they are his descendants.*

123 'Is this really true?'

antic round = *weird dance*

pernicious = *destructive*
133 'be cursed forever'

What is this so?

FIRST WITCH   Ay, sir, all this is so.   But why
   Stands Macbeth thus amazedly?   125
   Come, sisters, cheer we up his sprites,
   And show the best of our delights.
   I'll charm the air to give a sound,
   While you perform your antic round
   That this great king may kindly say,   130
   Our duties did his welcome pay.
                 Music. The WITCHES *dance, and vanish.*

MACBETH   Where are they? Gone? Let this pernicious hour,
   Stand aye accursèd in the calendar.
   Come in, without there!

                       Enter LENOX

LENOX   What's your grace's will?

135   That funny symbol means you
say it WEE-URD — like a Geordie.

MACBETH   Saw you the weïrd sisters?

LENOX   No, my lord.   135

MACBETH   Came they not by you?

LENOX   No indeed, my lord.

137 'I curse the air they fly through'

MACBETH   Infected be the air whereon they ride,
   And damned all those that trust them. I did hear
   The galloping of horse. Who was't came by?

LENOX   'Tis two or three, my lord, that bring you word   140
   Macduff is fled to England.

MACBETH   Fled to England?

LENOX   Ay, my good lord.

143-152 'I was too late to have him
killed. You never get to do what
you plan unless you do it straight
away. From now on I'll do things as
soon as I think of them. I'll have his
castle taken, and his family killed.'

MACBETH   *(Aside)* Time, thou anticipat'st my dread exploits.
   The flighty purpose never is o'ertook
   Unless the deed go with it. From this moment,   145
   The very firstlings of my heart shall be
   The firstlings of my hand. And even now,
   To crown my thoughts with acts, be it thought and done.
   The castle of Macduff I will surprise,
   Seize upon Fife, give to th'edge o'th'sword   150
   His wife, his babes, and all unfortunate souls
   That trace him in his line. No boasting like a fool,
   This deed I'll do before this purpose cool,
   But no more sights. — Where are these gentlemen?
   Come, bring me where they are.   155
                       Exeunt

Rosse has come to see Lady Macduff. They're discussing why Macduff's done a runner. Rosse leaves. Straight afterwards, murderers break in and kill Lady Macduff and all her children.

ACT 4 SCENE 2
Macduff's castle in Fife
Enter LADY MACDUFF, *her* SON, *and* ROSSE

fly = *escape*

2-4 'Macduff wasn't patient — he
was mad. He may not have **behaved**
like a traitor, but he was cowardly,
and that makes him a traitor.'

LADY MACDUFF   What had he done, to make him fly the land?

ROSSE   You must have patience, madam.

LADY MACDUFF   He had none —
   His flight was madness. When our actions do not,
   Our fears do make us traitors.

ROSSE   You know not
   Whether it was his wisdom or his fear.   5

LADY MACDUFF Wisdom! To leave his wife, to leave his babes,
   His mansion and his titles in a place
   From whence himself does fly? He loves us not,
   He wants the natural touch — for the poor wren,
   The most diminutive of birds, will fight,   10
   Her young ones in her nest, against the owl.
   All is the fear and nothing is the love,
   As little is the wisdom, where the flight
   So runs against all reason.

ROSSE   My dearest coz,
   I pray you, school yourself — but for your husband,   15
   He is noble, wise, judicious, and best knows
   The fits o' the season. I dare not speak much further,
   But cruel are the times, when we are traitors
   And do not know ourselves, when we hold rumour
   From what we fear, yet know not what we fear,   20
   But float upon a wild and violent sea
   Each way and move. I take my leave of you,
   Shall not be long but I'll be here again.
   Things at the worst will cease, or else climb upward
   To what they were before. *(to Son)* My pretty cousin,   25
   Blessing upon you!

LADY MACDUFF Fathered he is, and yet he's fatherless.

ROSSE I am so much a fool, should I stay longer,
   It would be my disgrace and your discomfort.
   I take my leave at once.

Exit

LADY MACDUFF   Sirrah, your father's dead;   30
   And what will you do now? How will you live?

SON As birds do, mother.

LADY MACDUFF   What, with worms and flies?

SON With what I get, I mean, and so do they.

LADY MACDUFF Poor bird! Thou'dst never fear the net nor lime,
   The pitfall nor the gin.   35

SON Why should I, mother? Poor birds they are not set for.
   My father is not dead, for all your saying.

LADY MACDUFF Yes, he is dead — how wilt thou do for a father?

SON Nay, how will you do for a husband?

LADY MACDUFF Why, I can buy me twenty at any market.   40

SON Then you'll buy 'em to sell again.

LADY MACDUFF Thou speak'st with all thy wit, and yet, i' faith,
   With wit enough for thee.

SON Was my father a traitor, mother?

LADY MACDUFF Ay, that he was.   45

SON What is a traitor?

LADY MACDUFF Why, one that swears and lies.

SON And be all traitors that do so?

---

whence = *where*

wants the natural touch = *behaved unnaturally*

9-11 *'The tiny wren will fight an owl to protect her young ones in the nest.'*

12-14 *'Running away doesn't make sense — it's cowardly, and shows no sign of love or wisdom.'*

school yourself = *calm down*

fits o' the season = *the troubles of the times*

19-20 *'We make up rumours based on our fears, even though we're not sure what it is we're afraid of'*

28-30 *'I'm off, before I cry and make a fool of myself.'*

30-31 *Macduff's not really dead. Lady Macduff's saying that because he's not here to protect her and the kids, he might as well be dead.*

33 *'I'll live on whatever comes my way.'*

net, lime, pitfall, gin = *different ways of trapping birds*

36 *'People only bother trapping rich birds, not poor ones.'*

Act 4, Scene 2

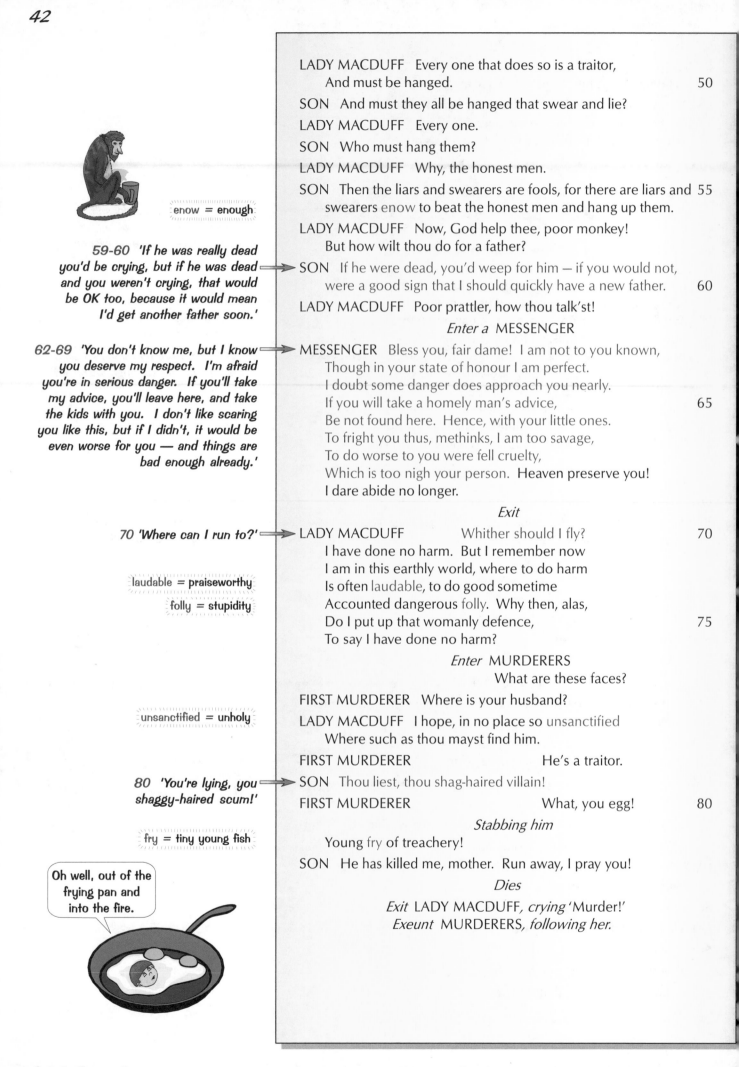

enow = enough

59-60 'If he was really dead you'd be crying, but if he was dead and you weren't crying, that would be OK too, because it would mean I'd get another father soon.'

62-69 'You don't know me, but I know you deserve my respect. I'm afraid you're in serious danger. If you'll take my advice, you'll leave here, and take the kids with you. I don't like scaring you like this, but if I didn't, it would be even worse for you — and things are bad enough already.'

70 'Where can I run to?'

laudable = praiseworthy

folly = stupidity

unsanctified = unholy

80 'You're lying, you shaggy-haired scum!'

fry = tiny young fish

Oh well, out of the frying pan and into the fire.

LADY MACDUFF   Every one that does so is a traitor,
   And must be hanged.   50

SON   And must they all be hanged that swear and lie?

LADY MACDUFF   Every one.

SON   Who must hang them?

LADY MACDUFF   Why, the honest men.

SON   Then the liars and swearers are fools, for there are liars and   55
   swearers enow to beat the honest men and hang up them.

LADY MACDUFF   Now, God help thee, poor monkey!
   But how wilt thou do for a father?

SON   If he were dead, you'd weep for him — if you would not,
   were a good sign that I should quickly have a new father.   60

LADY MACDUFF   Poor prattler, how thou talk'st!

Enter a MESSENGER

MESSENGER   Bless you, fair dame! I am not to you known,
   Though in your state of honour I am perfect.
   I doubt some danger does approach you nearly.
   If you will take a homely man's advice,   65
   Be not found here. Hence, with your little ones.
   To fright you thus, methinks, I am too savage,
   To do worse to you were fell cruelty,
   Which is too nigh your person. Heaven preserve you!
   I dare abide no longer.

Exit

LADY MACDUFF   Whither should I fly?   70
   I have done no harm. But I remember now
   I am in this earthly world, where to do harm
   Is often laudable, to do good sometime
   Accounted dangerous folly. Why then, alas,
   Do I put up that womanly defence,   75
   To say I have done no harm?

Enter MURDERERS
               What are these faces?

FIRST MURDERER   Where is your husband?

LADY MACDUFF   I hope, in no place so unsanctified
   Where such as thou mayst find him.

FIRST MURDERER   He's a traitor.

SON   Thou liest, thou shag-haired villain!

FIRST MURDERER   What, you egg!   80

Stabbing him

   Young fry of treachery!

SON   He has killed me, mother. Run away, I pray you!

Dies

Exit LADY MACDUFF, *crying* 'Murder!'
Exeunt MURDERERS, *following her.*

ACT 4 SCENE 3
England, the King's palace
Enter MALCOLM and MACDUFF

MALCOLM Let us seek out some desolate shade, and there
Weep our sad bosoms empty.

MACDUFF   Let us rather
Hold fast the mortal sword, and like good men
Bestride our down-fall'n birthdom. Each new morn
New widows howl, new orphans cry, new sorrows   5
Strike heaven on the face, that it resounds
As if it felt with Scotland and yelled out
Like syllable of dolour.

MALCOLM   What I believe I'll wail,
What know believe, and what I can redress,
As I shall find the time to friend, I will.   10
What you have spoke, it may be so perchance.
This tyrant, whose sole name blisters our tongues,
Was once thought honest. You have loved him well;
He hath not touched you yet. I am young, but something
You may deserve of him through me, and wisdom   15
To offer up a weak poor innocent lamb
To appease an angry god.

MACDUFF I am not treacherous.

MALCOLM   But Macbeth is.
A good and virtuous nature may recoil
In an imperial charge. But I shall crave your pardon, 20
That which you are my thoughts cannot transpose:
Angels are bright still, though the brightest fell;
Though all things foul would wear the brows of grace,
Yet grace must still look so.

MACDUFF   I have lost my hopes.

MALCOLM Perchance even there where I did find my doubts. 25
Why in that rawness left you wife and child,
Those precious motives, those strong knots of love,
Without leave-taking? I pray you,
Let not my jealousies be your dishonours,
But mine own safeties. You may be rightly just,   30
Whatever I shall think.

MACDUFF   Bleed, bleed, poor country!
Great tyranny! Lay thou thy basis sure,
For goodness dare not check thee. Wear thou thy wrongs,
The title is affeered! Fare thee well, lord —
I would not be the villain that thou think'st   35
For the whole space that's in the tyrant's grasp,
And the rich East to boot.

MALCOLM   Be not offended.
I speak not as in absolute fear of you.
I think our country sinks beneath the yoke.
It weeps, it bleeds; and each new day a gash   40
Is added to her wounds. I think withal
There would be hands uplifted in my right,
And here from gracious England have I offer

syllable of dolour = a cry of pain
redress = improve

2-4 'It would be better to take up our swords, and go and defend the country where we were born.'

11-13 'What you've said may be true, even though Macbeth was once believed to be honest.' This is where Malcolm starts testing Macduff by saying he distrusts him.

13-17 'You used to be his friend and he hasn't harmed you yet. I'm young, but you might want to kill me to keep Macbeth happy.'

imperial charge = massive cavalry charge in battle

20-21 'I'm sorry — I can't tell what you're really like.'

22 The brightest and best angel was Lucifer, who rebelled against God. He was thrown out of Heaven, and made his home in Hell. Malcolm's comparing Macbeth to Lucifer.

brows of grace = appearance of goodness

26-28 'How could you leave your wife and child in such a dangerous situation without even saying goodbye?'

28-30 'Don't be insulted — I just want to be sure I'm safe.'

32-33 'Just sit back and enjoy your dictatorship, Macbeth, because nobody good's going to stop you. Flaunt your wrong-doing — your position's secure.'

check = stop   affeered = secure

35-37 'I wouldn't be the scoundrel you think I am — not for the whole world.'

41-44 'I think I'd have support in Scotland, and I've been promised thousands of men by the English.'

44

44-49 Malcolm starts testing Macduff in a different way. He's pretending Scotland would be even worse off if he was king — he wants Macduff to disagree with him.

50-55 'I'm so evil that if you cut me open I'd be black inside, and Macbeth would seem innocent as a lamb.'

confineless = limitless

55-57 'There can't possibly be anyone more evil than Macbeth — not even in Hell.'

60-61 'There's no limit to my lust.'

63-65 'There's no obstacle that my lust could not overcome.'

boundless intemperance = complete inability to control yourself

70-72 'You can get away with it.'

73-76 'There are plenty of women willing to sleep with powerful men — you're not such an animal that all of them couldn't keep you happy.'

76-84 Malcolm says he's greedy for money as well as women.

stanchless avarice = limitless greed

forge quarrels = stir up arguments

foisons = riches

89-90 'These bad points are bearable if they're balanced against your good points.'

Of goodly thousands. But, for all this,
When I shall tread upon the tyrant's head,
Or wear it on my sword, yet my poor country
Shall have more vices than it had before,
More suffer and more sundry ways than ever,
By him that shall succeed.

MACDUFF   What should he be?

MALCOLM   It is myself I mean — in whom I know
All the particulars of vice so grafted
That, when they shall be opened, black Macbeth
Will seem as pure as snow, and the poor state
Esteem him as a lamb, being compared
With my confineless harms.

MACDUFF   Not in the legions
Of horrid hell can come a devil more damned
In evils to top Macbeth.

MALCOLM   I grant him bloody,
Luxurious, avaricious, false, deceitful,
Sudden, malicious, smacking of every sin
That has a name. But there's no bottom, none,
In my voluptuousness — your wives, your daughters,
Your matrons and your maids, could not fill up
The cistern of my lust, and my desire
All continent impediments would o'erbear
That did oppose my will. Better Macbeth
Than such an one to reign.

MACDUFF   Boundless intemperance
In nature is a tyranny. It hath been
The untimely emptying of the happy throne
And fall of many kings. But fear not yet
To take upon you what is yours — you may
Convey your pleasures in a spacious plenty,
And yet seem cold, the time you may so hoodwink.
We have willing dames enough. There cannot be
That vulture in you, to devour so many
As will to greatness dedicate themselves,
Finding it so inclined.

MALCOLM   With this there grows
In my most ill-composed affection such
A stanchless avarice that, were I king,
I should cut off the nobles for their lands,
Desire his jewels and this other's house:
And my more-having would be as a sauce
To make me hunger more, that I should forge
Quarrels unjust against the good and loyal,
Destroying them for wealth.

MACDUFF   This avarice
Sticks deeper, grows with more pernicious root
Than summer-seeming lust, and it hath been
The sword of our slain kings — yet do not fear;
Scotland hath foisons to fill up your will.
Of your mere own — all these are portable,
With other graces weighed.

45

50

55

60

65

70

75

80

85

90

Act 4, Scene 3

MALCOLM   But I have none. The king-becoming graces,
As justice, verity, temperance, stableness,
Bounty, perseverance, mercy, lowliness,
Devotion, patience, courage, fortitude,
I have no relish of them, but abound   95
In the division of each several crime,
Acting it many ways. Nay, had I power, I should
Pour the sweet milk of concord into hell,
Uproar the universal peace, confound
All unity on earth.

MACDUFF   O Scotland, Scotland!   100

MALCOLM   If such a one be fit to govern, speak —
I am as I have spoken.

MACDUFF   Fit to govern!
No, not to live. O nation miserable,
With an untitled tyrant bloody-sceptered,
When shalt thou see thy wholesome days again,   105
Since that the truest issue of thy throne
By his own interdiction stands accursed,
And does blaspheme his breed? Thy royal father
Was a most sainted king — the queen that bore thee,
Oftener upon her knees than on her feet,   110
Died every day she lived. Fare thee well!
These evils thou repeat'st upon thyself
Have banished me from Scotland. O my breast,
Thy hope ends here!

MALCOLM   Macduff, this noble passion,
Child of integrity, hath from my soul   115
Wiped the black scruples, reconciled my thoughts
To thy good truth and honour. Devilish Macbeth
By many of these trains hath sought to win me
Into his power, and modest wisdom plucks me
From over-credulous haste — but God above   120
Deal between thee and me! For even now
I put myself to thy direction, and
Unspeak mine own detraction, here abjure
The taints and blames I laid upon myself,
For strangers to my nature. I am yet   125
Unknown to woman, never was forsworn,
Scarcely have coveted what was mine own,
At no time broke my faith, would not betray
The devil to his fellow and delight
No less in truth than life. My first false speaking 130
Was this upon myself — what I am truly,
Is thine and my poor country's to command:
Whither indeed, before thy here-approach,
Old Siward, with ten thousand warlike men,
Already at a point, was setting forth.   135
Now we'll together; and the chance of goodness
Be like our warranted quarrel! Why are you silent?

MACDUFF   Such welcome and unwelcome things at once,
'Tis hard to reconcile.

Enter a DOCTOR

Act 4, Scene 3

91-97 Malcolm claims he hasn't got any of the good points kings are meant to have. He says he just does bad things in as many different ways as he can.

concord = peace, harmony

confound = put an end to

102-114 Macduff has a long rant saying there's no hope for Scotland as Malcolm's turned out to be so horrible.

106-108 'The true heir to the throne admits his own evils, and insults his own family.'

upon her knees = praying

112 'The terrible things you've said about yourself...'

114-117 'If you can get this worked up about what I've said you must be a decent bloke — I believe you're truthful and honourable.'

117-120 'Macbeth's been trying to win me over by offering me women and money, but I've been cautious.

121-130 'From now on I'll do as you advise. I take back all the bad stuff I said about myself. I'm a virgin, I've never lied, have never really even wanted my own stuff, I've never broken a promise, I wouldn't betray the devil, and I love truth as much as life itself.'

133-135 Even before Macduff arrived, Malcolm had been preparing an army to march on Scotland.

138-139 Malcolm's done a complete U-turn. He's gone from saying he's totally evil, to saying he wouldn't hurt a fly. Macduff doesn't know what to think.

46

the king = Edward the Confessor
(King of England 1042-1066)

141-145 'There's a crowd of wretched
people waiting for the King to cure
them. Medicine can't cure their disease,
but Edward's got a holy power to cure
— at his touch they soon get better.'

146-147 'The disease is
called "the evil" — it's a
miracle what he can do.'

swoln = swollen

stamp = medallion

benediction = blessing

158-159 Edward is an all-round holy
king. Shakespeare's describing a good
king to highlight how evil Macbeth is.

Rosse arrives. He slowly breaks the news
that Macduff's family has been killed.
Malcolm and Rosse persuade Macduff to
go and fight Macbeth for revenge.

162-163 'Hurry up God, and put a stop
to the problems that are preventing
people from seeing their friends.'

164 'Are things in Scotland
as bad as they were?'

166-173 'The only people you ever
see smiling have no idea what's going
on. Nobody pays any attention to
sighs and groans. Sorrow is the new
joy. If there's a funeral, nobody asks
who it's for. Good men die quicker
than the flowers in their caps.'

nice = detailed

176 'Every minute
something terrible happens.'

177 Rosse is stalling — he doesn't
know how to break the news.

MALCOLM   Well, more anon.
Comes the king forth, I pray you?   140

DOCTOR Ay, sir, there are a crew of wretched souls
That stay his cure — their malady convinces
The great assay of art, but at his touch,
Such sanctity hath heaven given his hand,
They presently amend.

MALCOLM   I thank you, doctor.   145

Exit DOCTOR

MACDUFF What's the disease he means?

MALCOLM   'Tis called the evil —
A most miraculous work in this good king,
Which often, since my here-remain in England,
I have seen him do. How he solicits heaven,
Himself best knows, but strangely-visited people,   150
All swoln and ulcerous, pitiful to the eye,
The mere despair of surgery, he cures,
Hanging a golden stamp about their necks,
Put on with holy prayers — and 'tis spoken,
To the succeeding royalty he leaves   155
The healing benediction. With this strange virtue,
He hath a heavenly gift of prophecy,
And sundry blessings hang about his throne,
That speak him full of grace.

Enter ROSSE

MACDUFF   See, who comes here?

MALCOLM My countryman, but yet I know him not.   160

MACDUFF My ever-gentle cousin, welcome hither.

MALCOLM I know him now. Good God, betimes remove
The means that makes us strangers!

ROSSE   Sir, amen.

MACDUFF Stands Scotland where it did?

ROSSE   Alas, poor country!
Almost afraid to know itself. It cannot   165
Be called our mother, but our grave, where nothing,
But who knows nothing, is once seen to smile,
Where sighs and groans and shrieks that rend the air
Are made, not marked, where violent sorrow seems
A modern ecstasy, the dead man's knell   170
Is there scarce asked for who, and good men's lives
Expire before the flowers in their caps,
Dying or ere they sicken.

MACDUFF   O, relation
Too nice, and yet too true!

MALCOLM   What's the newest grief?

ROSSE That of an hour's age doth hiss the speaker — 175
Each minute teems a new one.

MACDUFF   How does my wife?

ROSSE Why, well.

MACDUFF   And all my children?

Act 4, Scene 3

ROSSE   Well too.

MACDUFF   The tyrant has not battered at their peace?   ⟵   *178 'Macbeth hasn't harmed them?'*

ROSSE   No, they were well at peace when I did leave 'em.   ⟵   *179 'No, they were fine when I __left__.'*

MACDUFF   Be not a niggard of your speech — how goes't?   180

niggard = miser

ROSSE   When I came hither to transport the tidings,
   Which I have heavily borne, there ran a rumour   ⟵   *182-185 'There was a rumour that some good men had gone into open rebellion. I'm sure it was true because I saw some of Macbeth's forces out too.'*
   Of many worthy fellows that were out,
   Which was to my belief witnessed the rather,
   For that I saw the tyrant's power afoot: 185
   Now is the time of help. Your eye in Scotland   ⟵   *186-188 'If you were in Scotland you'd inspire people to fight — even the women would fight to rid themselves of their troubles.'*
   Would create soldiers, make our women fight,
   To doff their dire distresses.

MALCOLM   Be't their comfort
   We are coming thither — gracious England hath
   Lent us good Siward and ten thousand men;   190
   An older and a better soldier none
   That Christendom gives out.

ROSSE   Would I could answer   ⟵   *192-193 'I wish I had some good news to tell in return.'*
   This comfort with the like! But I have words
   That would be howled out in the desert air,
   Where hearing should not latch them.

latch = catch

MACDUFF   What concern they?   195
   The general cause? Or is it a fee-grief   ⟵   *196-197 'Or is it news that would only be sad to one person?'*
   Due to some single breast?

ROSSE   No mind that's honest   ⟵   *197-199 'It would make any decent person feel bad, but mainly it's bad news for you.'*
   But in it shares some woe, though the main part
   Pertains to you alone.

MACDUFF   If it be mine,
   Keep it not from me, quickly let me have it.   200

ROSSE   Let not your ears despise my tongue for ever,   ⟵   *201-203 'I hope you're not going to hate me for giving you the worst news you've ever had.'*
   Which shall possess them with the heaviest sound
   That ever yet they heard.

MACDUFF   H'm! I guess at it.

ROSSE   Your castle is surprised, your wife and babes

surprised = captured

   Savagely slaughtered — to relate the manner,   205   ⟵   *205-207 'if I told you exactly what had happened it would be the end of you too.'*
   Were, on the quarry of these murdered deer,
   To add the death of you.

MALCOLM   Merciful heaven!
   What, man! Ne'er pull your hat upon your brows,   ⟵   *208-210 'Let it all out — if you hide your feelings, they'll overflow and break your heart.'*
   Give sorrow words — the grief that does not speak
   Whispers the o'er-fraught heart and bids it break.   210

MACDUFF   My children too?

ROSSE   Wife, children, servants, all
   That could be found.

MACDUFF   And I must be from thence!
   My wife killed too?

ROSSE   I have said.

MALCOLM   Be comforted:
   Let's make us medicines of our great revenge,   ⟵   *214-215 'We can cure our grief by taking revenge.'*
   To cure this deadly grief.

48

215 *Macbeth hasn't got any kids. Macduff can't have complete revenge if he can't kill Macbeth's children.*

219 *'Be a man — fight against it.'*

219-220 *Macduff says he'll fight like a man, but it's also a natural human reaction to be upset.*

224-226 *'I should have been killed, not them. They died because of my wrongdoing — not their own.'*

whetstone = sharpener

229-231 *'I could cry and boast, but there's no time for delay.'*

front to front = face to face

236-238 *'The only thing we still need to do is say goodbye to Edward. Macbeth's like a ripe apple, ready to fall from the tree. The gods are with us.'*

MACDUFF   He has no children.
All my pretty ones? Did you say all?
O hell-kite! All? What, all my pretty chickens
And their dam at one fell swoop?

MALCOLM   Dispute it like a man.

MACDUFF   I shall do so,
But I must also feel it as a man.
I cannot but remember such things were,
That were most precious to me. Did heaven look on,
And would not take their part? Sinful Macduff,
They were all struck for thee! Naught that I am,
Not for their own demerits, but for mine,
Fell slaughter on their souls. Heaven rest them now!

MALCOLM   Be this the whetstone of your sword — let grief
Convert to anger. Blunt not the heart, enrage it.

MACDUFF   O, I could play the woman with mine eyes
And braggart with my tongue! But, gentle heavens,
Cut short all intermission. Front to front
Bring thou this fiend of Scotland and myself.
Within my sword's length set him.   If he 'scape,
Heaven forgive him too!

MALCOLM   This tune goes manly.
Come, go we to the king, our power is ready,
Our lack is nothing but our leave. Macbeth
Is ripe for shaking, and the powers above
Put on their instruments. Receive what cheer you may:
The night is long that never finds the day.

Exeunt

215

220

225

230

235

Act 4, Scene 3

Act 4 — Revision Summary

It ain't good enough just to know the general plot of the story — you've really got to get to grips with Shakespeare's arty-farty language to be able to answer questions on the play well. Use these questions to give you in-depth knowledge of Act 4. You know the score by now — use the book to help you at first, then keep going over them until you don't need to look back any more.

1) Name ten things the witches put into their magic potion in <u>Act 4, Scene 1</u>.

2) Who is Hecate? Why is she annoyed at the three witches?

3) What do the witches mean when they tell the apparitions to "Thyself and office deftly show"?

4) What do the three apparitions look like? What does each one tell Macbeth?

5) What does Macbeth plan to "make assurance double sure" of?

6) What is the "round and top of sovereignty"?

7) What are "hautboys"?   a) male servants
                            b) drums
                            c) wind instruments

8) What is the last of the eight ghost kings carrying? What does Macbeth see in it?

9) Write down the exact words that Macbeth uses to curse the witches when they vanish.

10) What does Lenox come to tell Macbeth? What is Macbeth's reaction to this?

11) In <u>Act 4, Scene 2</u>, why does Lady Macduff think that her husband is a traitor?

12) Where is Macduff's castle?

13) What does Rosse mean when he says "It would be my disgrace and your discomfort"?

14) What does Macduff junior compare himself to? Why doesn't he fear being 'trapped'?

15) What is the cheeky young tyke saying in lines 58-59?

16) What does the messenger come to tell Lady Macduff?

17) Translate "Whither should I fly?" into normal English.

18) Write down all the insulting names that the Son and the Murderer call each other.

19) In <u>Act 4, Scene 3</u>, is a "syllable of dolour":
    a) a sigh, or
    b) a cry of pain?

20) What is Malcolm implying when he compares himself to a "weak poor innocent lamb"?

21) Rewrite "That which you are my thoughts cannot transpose" in modern English.

22) What two main faults does Malcolm pretend he has when he's talking to Macduff?

23) What words does Macduff use to say that these faults are OK when balanced against Malcolm's good points?

24) Why has Malcolm been lying to Macduff about himself?

25) What has Malcolm already done to help Scotland fight against Macbeth?

26) What is Macduff saying in lines 138-9?

27) What special power does the doctor say that King Edward has?

28) Who comes to tell Macduff that his family's been killed? How does he stall for time?

29) What does Malcolm mean when he tells Macduff to "Ne'er pull your hat upon your brows"?

30) What words show that Macduff blames himself for the murders of his wife and kids?

31) What's the only thing they've got left to do, before going off to fight in Scotland?

Lady Macbeth has gone a bit loopy and has taken to sleepwalking and talking nonsense. Her mad ramblings have been brought on by her guilt about the murders she's been involved in: Duncan's, Lady Macduff's and Banquo's.

ACT 5 SCENE 1
A room in Dunsinane castle.

Enter a DOCTOR and a WAITING-GENTLEWOMAN.

DOCTOR I have two nights watched with you, but can perceive no truth in your report. When was it she last walked?

GENTLEWOMAN Since his majesty went into the field, I have seen her rise from her bed, throw her night-gown upon her, unlock her closet, take forth paper, fold it, write upon't, read   5
it, afterwards seal it, and again return to bed; yet all this while in a most fast sleep.

field = battlefield

3-7 Lady Macbeth's been doing a whole lot of sleep-walking.

perturbation in nature = physical disorder

watching = being awake

slumbery agitation = sleepwalking

DOCTOR A great perturbation in nature, to receive at once the benefit of sleep, and do the effects of watching! In this slumbery agitation, besides her walking and other actual   10
performances, what, at any time, have you heard her say?

11 'What has she been saying?'

GENTLEWOMAN That, sir, which I will not report after her.

12 'I'm not telling you.'

DOCTOR You may to me, and 'tis most meet you should.

13 'You can tell me — and it's best that you do.'

GENTLEWOMAN Neither to you nor any one; having no witness to confirm my speech.   15

Enter LADY MACBETH, with a taper.

taper = candle

Lo you, here she comes! This is her very guise — and, upon my life, fast asleep. Observe her; stand close.

16 'Here she comes. This is what she always does.'

DOCTOR How came she by that light?

18 'How come she's got that candle?'

GENTLEWOMAN Why, it stood by her — she has light by her continually. 'Tis her command.   20

19-20 'She's ordered that there should always be one next to her.' (Probably she's scared of the dark now.)

DOCTOR You see, her eyes are open.

GENTLEWOMAN Ay, but their sense is shut.

22 'But they're not seeing anything.'

DOCTOR What is it she does now? Look, how she rubs her hands.

GENTLEWOMAN It is an accustomed action with her, to seem thus washing her hands — I have known her continue in this a   25
quarter of an hour.

24-26 'She's always washing her hands like this. I've seen her do it for 15 mins before.'

LADY MACBETH Yet here's a spot.

DOCTOR Hark! she speaks — I will set down what comes from her, to satisfy my remembrance the more strongly.

28-29 'I'll write down what she says, so I don't forget.'

LADY MACBETH Out, damned spot! Out, I say! One: two: 30
why, then, 'tis time to do't. Hell is murky! Fie, my lord, fie! a soldier, and afeard? What need we fear who knows it, when none can call our power to account? — Yet who would have thought the old man to have had so much blood in him.   35

30 She's trying to wash 'spots' of imagined blood off her hands.

32-33 'It doesn't matter if people know what we've done, because we're king and queen so we can do what we like.'

the old man = Duncan

DOCTOR Do you mark that?

LADY MACBETH The Thane of Fife had a wife — where is she now? What, will these hands ne'er be clean? No more o' that, my lord, no more o' that: you mar all with this starting.

37-38 Now she's feeling guilty about Lady Macduff's murder (the Thane of Fife's wife).

39 'Macbeth, you've ruined everything with your nervousness.'

DOCTOR Go to, go to — you have known what you should not.   40

GENTLEWOMAN She has spoke what she should not, I am sure of that — heaven knows what she has known.

LADY MACBETH Here's the smell of the blood still — all the perfumes of Arabia will not sweeten this little hand. O, o, o!

DOCTOR What a sigh is there! The heart is sorely charged.   45

the heart is sorely charged = she has a heavy heart

GENTLEWOMAN I would not have such a heart in my bosom
  for the dignity of the whole body.

46-47 'I wouldn't want to feel like she does for all the world.'

DOCTOR Well, well, well, —

GENTLEWOMAN Pray God it be, sir.

DOCTOR This disease is beyond my practice, yet I have known   50
  those which have walked in their sleep who have died holily
  in their beds.

LADY MACBETH Wash your hands, put on your nightgown — look
  not so pale. I tell you yet again, Banquo's buried; he cannot
  come out on's grave.   55

53-55 Now she's talking about Banquo's murder.

I confess — it was me.

DOCTOR Even so?

LADY MACBETH To bed, to bed! there's knocking at the gate.
  Come, come, come, come, give me your hand. What's done
  cannot be undone. To bed, to bed, to bed.

Exit

DOCTOR Will she go now to bed?   60

GENTLEWOMAN Directly.

DOCTOR Foul whisperings are abroad — unnatural deeds
  Do breed unnatural troubles, infected minds
  To their deaf pillows will discharge their secrets.
  More needs she the divine than the physician.   65
  God, God forgive us all! Look after her;
  Remove from her the means of all annoyance,
  And still keep eyes upon her. So, good night:
  My mind she has mated, and amazed my sight.
  I think, but dare not speak.   70

62-65 'I've heard some nasty rumours. Minds that are turned bad by evil have to confess — even if it's only to their pillows. The doctor can't help her — she needs a priest.'

mated = confused

GENTLEWOMAN Good night, good doctor.

Exeunt

ACT 5 SCENE 2
Open country near Dunsinane

*Drum and colours. Enter MENTEITH, CAITHNESS,
ANGUS, LENOX, and Soldiers.*

The Scottish Thanes are talking about the arrival of the English army and how unpopular Macbeth is now. Malcolm is dead popular and loads of people are supporting him.

colours = flags

MENTEITH The English power is near, led on by Malcolm,
  His uncle Siward and the good Macduff.
  Revenges burn in them, for their dear causes
  Would to the bleeding and the grim alarm
  Excite the mortified man.

1-5 'The English armies are approaching, led by Malcolm, Siward and Macduff. They're burning with revenge, because the things they've suffered are enough to wake the dead.'

ANGUS   Near Birnam wood   5
  Shall we well meet them; that way are they coming.

5-6 'We'll meet them at Birnam wood.'

CAITHNESS Who knows if Donalbain be with his brother?

LENOX For certain, sir, he is not. I have a file
  Of all the gentry — there is Siward's son,
  And many unrough youths that even now   10
  Protest their first of manhood.

file = list

unrough = unbearded

10-11 Lots of inexperienced young men have joined the English armies for battle.

MENTEITH   What does the tyrant?

11 'What's Macbeth doing about it?'

CAITHNESS Great Dunsinane he strongly fortifies.

52

13-14 *'Some people think Macbeth's mad. The ones that don't hate him so much think he's in a right temper.'*
distempered cause = *rebellious kingdom*

Some say he's mad, others that lesser hate him
Do call it valiant fury, but for certain,
He cannot buckle his distempered cause
Within the belt of rule.   15

ANGUS   Now does he feel
His secret murders sticking on his hands,

18-20 *'Every minute there's a rebellion against his treason. His soldiers obey him through fear, not love.'*
faith-breach = *treason*

pestered = *troubled*

Now minutely revolts upbraid his faith-breach —
Those he commands move only in command,
Nothing in love. Now does he feel his title   20
Hang loose about him, like a giant's robe
Upon a dwarfish thief.

MENTEITH   Who then shall blame
His pestered senses to recoil and start,
When all that is within him does condemn
Itself for being there?

26-29 *'We'll obey Malcolm, and the blood we shed will help to cure our country.'*
the med'cine of the sickly weal = *Malcolm*
purge = *cure by cleansing*
dew the sovereign flower = *restore the rightful king*

CAITHNESS   Well, march we on,   25
To give obedience where 'tis truly owed.
Meet we the med'cine of the sickly weal,
And with him pour we in our country's purge
Each drop of us.

LENOX   Or so much as it needs
To dew the sovereign flower and drown the weeds.   30
Make we our march towards Birnam.

Exeunt, marching.

Macbeth hears about the approaching army but isn't scared because of the predictions the apparitions made. The doctor tells him he can't cure Lady Macbeth's disease.

ACT 5 SCENE 3
A room in Dunsinane castle

Enter MACBETH, DOCTOR, *and Attendants.*

MACBETH Bring me no more reports. Let them fly all;

2-7 *'I won't be worried until Birnam wood comes to the castle. I'm not scared of Malcolm — a woman gave birth to him and the apparitions said I shouldn't fear anyone whose mum was a woman.'*
epicures = *people who like luxury*

Till Birnam wood remove to Dunsinane,
I cannot taint with fear. What's the boy Malcolm?
Was he not born of woman? The spirits that know
All mortal consequences have pronounced me thus: 5
'Fear not, Macbeth, no man that's born of woman
Shall e'er have power upon thee.' Then fly, false thanes,
And mingle with the English epicures.
The mind I sway by and the heart I bear
Shall never sag with doubt nor shake with fear.   10

Enter a SERVANT

11-17 *Macbeth's being really rude to the servant, teasing him for being a cowardy-custard.*
loon = *rascal*
lily-livered = *cowardly*
patch = *fool*
linen cheeks = *pale cheeks*
whey-face = *pale face*

The devil damn thee black, thou cream-faced loon!
Where got'st thou that goose look?

SERVANT There is ten thousand —

MACBETH   Geese, villain?

SERVANT   Soldiers, sir.

MACBETH Go prick thy face, and over-red thy fear,
Thou lily-livered boy. What soldiers, patch?   15
Death of thy soul, those linen cheeks of thine
Are counsellors to fear. What soldiers, whey-face?

SERVANT The English force, so please you.

MACBETH Take thy face hence.

Exit SERVANT

Act 5, Scene 3

Seyton! — I am sick at heart, 20
When I behold — Seyton, I say! — This push
Will cheer me ever, or disseat me now.
I have lived long enough — my way of life
Is fall'n into the sere, the yellow leaf,
And that which should accompany old age, 25
As honour, love, obedience, troops of friends,
I must not look to have; but, in their stead,
Curses, not loud but deep, mouth-honour, breath,
Which the poor heart would fain deny, and dare not.
Seyton! 30

Enter SEYTON

SEYTON   What is your gracious pleasure?

MACBETH   What news more?

SEYTON   All is confirmed, my lord, which was reported.

MACBETH   I'll fight till from my bones my flesh be hacked.
Give me my armour.

SEYTON   'Tis not needed yet.

MACBETH   I'll put it on. 35
Send out more horses, skirr the country round,
Hang those that talk of fear. Give me mine armour.
How does your patient, doctor?

DOCTOR   Not so sick, my lord,
As she is troubled with thick coming fancies,
That keep her from her rest.

MACBETH   Cure her of that. 40
Canst thou not minister to a mind diseased,
Pluck from the memory a rooted sorrow,
Raze out the written troubles of the brain
And with some sweet oblivious antidote
Cleanse the stuffed bosom of that perilous stuff 45
Which weighs upon the heart?

DOCTOR   Therein the patient
Must minister to himself.

MACBETH   Throw physic to the dogs — I'll none of it.
Come, put mine armour on, give me my staff.
Seyton, send out. Doctor, the thanes fly from me. 50
Come, sir, dispatch. If thou couldst, doctor, cast
The water of my land, find her disease,
And purge it to a sound and pristine health,
I would applaud thee to the very echo,
That should applaud again. Pull't off, I say. 55
What rhubarb, cyme, or what purgative drug,
Would scour these English hence? Hear'st thou of them?

DOCTOR   Ay, my good lord; your royal preparation
Makes us hear something.

MACBETH   Bring it after me.
I will not be afraid of death and bane, 60
Till Birnam forest come to Dunsinane.

DOCTOR   *(Aside)* Were I from Dunsinane away and clear,
Profit again should hardly draw me here.

Exeunt

21-22 'This battle will either cheer me up or dethrone me.'
23-29 'I'm getting old and, instead of love and obedience, all I get is curses and flattery.'
sere = withered state
mouth-honour = flattery
fain = gladly
33 'I'm going to fight to the bitter end.'
skirr = scour
37-38 'Hang any scare-mongers. Give me my armour. How's my wife, doctor?'
thick coming fancies = frequent nightmares
41-46 'Surely you can cure her by removing the troubles from her brain with some kind of medicine?'
46-47 'Only she can help herself.'
48 'Medicine is a load of old cobblers, then.'
51-55 'Doctor, if you could find a cure for Scotland's disease I'd be well chuffed.'
cast the water = test the urine
pristine = fresh
purgative = cleansing
bane = ruin
62-63 'I'm not coming back to this crazy place in a hurry.'

The English army is organising itself for battle. Malcolm tells everyone to cut down a branch from Birnam wood and hide behind it. They discuss rumours of desertion in Macbeth's army.

colours = battle flags

ACT 5 SCENE 4
Open country near Birnam wood

Drum and colours. Enter MALCOLM, SIWARD and YOUNG SIWARD, MACDUFF, MENTEITH, CAITHNESS, ANGUS, LENOX, ROSSE, and Soldiers, marching.

1-2 'Soon we'll be able to sleep sound in our beds again.'

MALCOLM   Cousins, I hope the days are near at hand
That chambers will be safe.

MENTEITH   We doubt it nothing.

SIWARD   What wood is this before us?

MENTEITH   The wood of Birnam.

4-7 'Everyone cut down a branch and hide behind it — so the enemy can't tell how many of us there are.'

MALCOLM   Let every soldier hew him down a bough
And bear't before him — thereby shall we shadow   5
The numbers of our host and make discovery
Err in report of us.

SOLDIERS   It shall be done.

8-10 'All we know is that Macbeth is waiting for us to lay siege to his castle.'

SIWARD   We learn no other but the confident tyrant
Keeps still in Dunsinane, and will endure
Our setting down before 't.

10-14 'That's the best he can do, because his men are deserting him, and the ones that are left are unwilling.'

MALCOLM   'Tis his main hope,   10
For where there is advantage to be given,
Both more and less have given him the revolt,
And none serve with him but constrainèd things
Whose hearts are absent too.

more and less = nobles and ordinary men

14-16 'Let's save our opinions for after the battle and concentrate on being good soldiers.'

MACDUFF   Let our just censures
Attend the true event, and put we on   15
Industrious soldiership.

SIWARD   The time approaches
That will with due decision make us know
What we shall say we have and what we owe.
Thoughts speculative their unsure hopes relate,
But certain issue strokes must arbitrate —   20
Towards which advance the war.

Exeunt, marching

Macbeth is waiting for the English army to lay siege — he's still not scared. He finds out that Lady Macbeth is dead. Then, a messenger tells him Birnam wood is coming towards the castle. He decides to go out and fight the army.

ACT 5   SCENE 5
Inside Dunsinane castle

Enter MACBETH, SEYTON, and Soldiers, with drum and colours

2-6 'The English army is coming. Let them wait in siege until they all die of hunger and disease. We'd fight them face-to-face if they didn't have so many reinforcements — I wanted those men to fight for me.'

MACBETH   Hang out our banners on the outward walls.
The cry is still 'They come!' Our castle's strength
Will laugh a siege to scorn — here let them lie
Till famine and the ague eat them up.
Were they not forced with those that should be ours,   5
We might have met them dareful, beard to beard,
And beat them backward home.

A cry of women within
                          What is that noise?

SEYTON   It is the cry of women, my good lord.

ague = fever

forced = reinforced

Exit

MACBETH I have almost forgot the taste of fears;
    The time has been, my senses would have cooled   10
    To hear a night-shriek, and my fell of hair
    Would at a dismal treatise rouse and stir
    As life were in't: I have supped full with horrors;
    Direness, familiar to my slaughterous thoughts,
    Cannot once start me.

Re-enter SEYTON
                Wherefore was that cry?   15

SEYTON The queen, my lord, is dead.

MACBETH She should have died hereafter,
    There would have been a time for such a word.
    To-morrow, and to-morrow, and to-morrow,
    Creeps in this petty pace from day to day   20
    To the last syllable of recorded time,
    And all our yesterdays have lighted fools
    The way to dusty death. Out, out, brief candle!
    Life's but a walking shadow, a poor player
    That struts and frets his hour upon the stage   25
    And then is heard no more. It is a tale
    Told by an idiot, full of sound and fury,
    Signifying nothing.

Enter a MESSENGER
    Thou comest to use thy tongue, thy story quickly.

MESSENGER Gracious my lord,   30
    I should report that which I say I saw,
    But know not how to do it.

MACBETH   Well, say, sir.

MESSENGER As I did stand my watch upon the hill,
    I looked toward Birnam, and anon, methought,
    The wood began to move.

MACBETH   Liar and slave!   35

MESSENGER Let me endure your wrath, if't be not so.
    Within this three mile may you see it coming;
    I say, a moving grove.

MACBETH   If thou speak'st false,
    Upon the next tree shalt thou hang alive,
    Till famine cling thee — if thy speech be sooth,   40
    I care not if thou dost for me as much.
    I pull in resolution, and begin
    To doubt the equivocation of the fiend
    That lies like truth: 'Fear not, till Birnam wood
    Do come to Dunsinane,' and now a wood   45
    Comes toward Dunsinane. Arm, arm, and out!
    If this which he avouches does appear,
    There is nor flying hence nor tarrying here.
    I gin to be aweary of the sun,
    And wish the estate o' the world were now undone.   50
    Ring the alarum-bell! Blow, wind! Come, wrack!
    At least we'll die with harness on our back.

Exeunt

9-15 'I've almost forgotten what it's like to be scared. I used to be scared of night-time noises, and my hair stood on end at spooky stories. But now I'm used to horror and nothing can scare me.'

fell of hair = *hair on skin*

treatise = *story*

17-28 Macbeth ponders on the pointlessness of life. He says that endless days all merge together until we die — it doesn't mean anything.

29 'Say what you've got to say quickly!'

watch = *guard duty*

wrath = *anger*

grove = *wood*

38-44 'I'll hang you if you're lying — and if you're telling the truth, you can hang me, for all I care. I'm not so sure the apparition *was* telling the truth about Birnam wood now.'

sooth = *true*

Uh-oh!

avouches = *says is true*

tarrying = *waiting*

estate o' the world = *universe*

harness = *armour*

Act 5, Scene 5

Malcolm orders the army to throw down their tree branches as they near the castle. He gives out orders for the battle.

ACT 5 SCENE 6
Outside Dunsinane castle

Drum and colours. Enter MALCOLM, SIWARD, MACDUFF, and their Army, with boughs.

1-2 'Throw down your branches and let them see how many of us there are.'

MALCOLM Now near enough — your leafy screens throw down.
And show like those you are. You, worthy uncle,
Shall, with my cousin, your right-noble son,
Lead our first battle. Worthy Macduff and we
Shall take upon's what else remains to do,   5
According to our order.

SIWARD   Fare you well.
Do we but find the tyrant's power to-night,

8 'We'll fight to the end.'
Let us be beaten, if we cannot fight.

9-10 Macduff orders the trumpets to announce the start of battle.

MACDUFF Make all our trumpets speak, give them all breath,
Those clamorous harbingers of blood and death.   10

clamorous harbingers = noisy announcers

Exeunt

Macbeth kills Siward's son in battle. Macduff's looking for Macbeth — he wants to be the one to kill him. Siward reports to Malcolm that the battle's turning his way.

ACT 5 SCENE 7
The battlefield outside the castle

Alarums. Enter MACBETH.

1-2 'Like a baited bear, I can't run away — I'll have to stay and fight.'

MACBETH   They have tied me to a stake, I cannot fly,
But, bear-like, I must fight the course. What's he
That was not born of woman? Such a one
Am I to fear, or none.

Enter YOUNG SIWARD

YOUNG SIWARD   What is thy name?

MACBETH   Thou'lt be afraid to hear it. 5

6-7 'No I won't!'

YOUNG SIWARD No, though thou call'st thyself a hotter name
Than any is in hell.

Nitwit

MACBETH   My name's Macbeth.

YOUNG SIWARD The devil himself could not pronounce a title
More hateful to mine ear.

MACBETH   No, nor more fearful.

abhorrèd = hated

YOUNG SIWARD Thou liest, abhorrèd tyrant. With my sword   10
I'll prove the lie thou speak'st.

They fight and YOUNG SIWARD is slain

11-13 'I'm not scared of weapons held by anyone born of a woman!'

brandished = held

MACBETH   Thou wast born of woman
But swords I smile at, weapons laugh to scorn,
Brandished by man that's of a woman born.

Exit

Alarums. Enter MACDUFF

15-20 'If anyone else but me kills you, I'll still be haunted by my family's ghosts. I'm not fighting any old soldiers — if I can't kill you, then I won't use my sword.'

kerns = soldiers

staves = wooden spears

MACDUFF That way the noise is. Tyrant, show thy face!
If thou be'st slain and with no stroke of mine,   15
My wife and children's ghosts will haunt me still.
I cannot strike at wretched kerns, whose arms
Are hired to bear their staves — either thou, Macbeth,

Or else my sword with an unbattered edge
I sheathe again undeeded. There thou shouldst be,   20
By this great clatter, one of greatest note
Seems bruited. Let me find him, fortune!
And more I beg not.

Exit. Alarums

Enter MALCOLM *and* SIWARD

SIWARD   This way, my lord. The castle's gently rendered —
The tyrant's people on both sides do fight,   25
The noble Thanes do bravely in the war,
The day almost itself professes yours,
And little is to do.

MALCOLM   We have met with foes
That strike beside us.

SIWARD   Enter, sir, the castle.

Exeunt. Alarums

undeeded = *unused*

bruited = *announced*

gently rendered = *surrendered quietly*

25-28 'Some of Macbeth's army have joined our side. The Thanes are fighting well and we've almost won the battle.'

ACT 5 SCENE 8
Another part of the field

Enter MACBETH

MACBETH   Why should I play the Roman fool, and die
On mine own sword? Whiles I see lives, the gashes
Do better upon them.

Enter MACDUFF

MACDUFF   Turn, hell-hound, turn!

MACBETH   Of all men else I have avoided thee —
But get thee back, my soul is too much charged   5
With blood of thine already.

MACDUFF   I have no words:
My voice is in my sword, thou bloodier villain
Than terms can give thee out!

They fight.

MACBETH   Thou losest labour.
As easy mayst thou the intrenchant air
With thy keen sword impress as make me bleed.   10
Let fall thy blade on vulnerable crests,
I bear a charmèd life, which must not yield,
To one of woman born.

MACDUFF   Despair thy charm,
And let the angel whom thou still hast served
Tell thee, Macduff was from his mother's womb   15
Untimely ripped.

MACBETH   Accursèd be that tongue that tells me so,
For it hath cowed my better part of man!
And be these juggling fiends no more believed,
That palter with us in a double sense,   20
That keep the word of promise to our ear,
And break it to our hope. I'll not fight with thee.

Macbeth and Macduff finally meet face to face in the battle. Macbeth is sure he'll win, until he finds out Macduff wasn't born of a woman. They fight and Macbeth is killed.

1-2 Romans thought it was better to commit suicide than be dishonoured.

5-6 'Get back — I've shed enough blood in your family already.'

6-7 'I can't speak, I can only fight you.'

terms = *words*

8-13 'You're wasting your time. You can't hurt me, just as you can't cut the air with your sword. Go and fight normal soldiers, because I'm special and can't be killed by anyone born of a woman.'

intrenchant = *uncuttable*

13-16 'Best check the small-print, mate — I was born by Caesarian section.'

untimely ripped = *delivered by Caesarian section*

17-22 'Oh no, I'm scared now. Those apparitions were lying, with their double meanings and false promises.'

cowed = *frightened*

palter = *talk insincerely*

23-27 'We'll put you in a freak show, so everyone can come and see the tyrant for themselves.'

underwrit = written underneath

MACDUFF Then yield thee, coward,
And live to be the show and gaze o' the time.
We'll have thee, as our rarer monsters are,   25
Painted on a pole, and underwrit,
'Here may you see the tyrant.'

27-29 'I'm not giving in, to grovel at Malcolm's feet and be mocked by everyone.'

MACBETH   I will not yield,
To kiss the ground before young Malcolm's feet,
And to be baited with the rabble's curse.
Though Birnam wood be come to Dunsinane,   30
And thou opposed, being of no woman born,

32 'I'll fight to the end.'

Yet I will try the last. Before my body
I throw my warlike shield. Lay on, Macduff,
And damned be him that first cries, 'Hold, enough!'

                              Exeunt, fighting. Alarums

Siward finds out that his son was killed by Macbeth, but doesn't seem to mind too much because he died bravely. Macduff arrives, carrying Macbeth's head. Malcolm is made the new king and they all give each other a pat on the back.

ACT 5 SCENE 9
Inside Dunsinane Castle

Retreat. Flourish.

*Enter, with drum and colours, MALCOLM, SIWARD,
ROSSE, the other Thanes, and Soldiers.*

MALCOLM I would the friends we miss were safe arrived.

2-3 'Some people are bound to die, but not many by the look of things.'

SIWARD Some must go off— and yet, by these I see,
So great a day as this is cheaply bought.

MALCOLM Macduff is missing, and your noble son.

paid a soldier's debt = died

ROSSE Your son, my lord, has paid a soldier's debt.   5
He only lived but till he was a man,
The which no sooner had his prowess confirmed

prowess = bravery

In the unshrinking station where he fought,
But like a man he died.

SIWARD   Then he is dead?

ROSSE Ay, and brought off the field — your cause of sorrow   15
Must not be measured by his worth, for then
It hath no end.

17 'Were his wounds on the front of his body?'

SIWARD   Had he his hurts before?

ROSSE Ay, on the front.

18-20 Siward is pleased his son's injuries are on his front because it shows he didn't run away, but faced his enemy.

SIWARD   Why then, God's soldier be he!
Had I as many sons as I have hairs,
I would not wish them to a fairer death: 20

21 'So, his death bell is rung.'

And so, his knell is knolled.

MALCOLM   He's worth more sorrow,
And that I'll spend for him.

SIWARD   He's worth no more;
They say he parted well, and paid his score.
And so, God be with him! Here comes newer comfort.

                    Re-enter MACDUFF, with MACBETH's head

usurper = thief of the crown

MACDUFF Hail, king! For so thou art — behold, where stands   25
The usurper's cursèd head. The time is free.

I see thee compassed with thy kingdom's pearl,
That speak my salutation in their minds,
Whose voices I desire aloud with mine:
Hail, King of Scotland!

ALL   Hail, King of Scotland!   30

Flourish

MALCOLM   We shall not spend a large expense of time
    Before we reckon with your several loves,
    And make us even with you. My Thanes and kinsmen,
    Henceforth be Earls, the first that ever Scotland
    In such an honour named. What's more to do,   35
    Which would be planted newly with the time,
    As calling home our exiled friends abroad
    That fled the snares of watchful tyranny,
    Producing forth the cruel ministers
    Of this dead butcher and his fiend-like queen,   40
    Who, as 'tis thought, by self and violent hands
    Took off her life; this, and what needful else
    That calls upon us, by the grace of Grace,
    We will perform in measure, time and place.
    So, thanks to all at once and to each one,   45
    Whom we invite to see us crowned at Scone.

Flourish. Exeunt

27-30 'I see you're surrounded by Scotland's nobility, and I'm sure they're thinking the same thing as me. I want them all to say with me: Hail, King of Scotland.'

reckon with your separate loves = give each of you a reward

33-35 'For now, I'm going to make you into the first Earls that Scotland has had.'

35-40 Malcolm promises to bring back to Scotland everyone who ran away from Macbeth's tyranny (e.g. Donalbain) and to find those that helped Macbeth (e.g. the Murderers).

producing forth = finding

41-42 Lady Macbeth committed suicide.

45-46 He invites everyone to his coronation in Scone.

I've finally got something to smile about!

Act 5, Scene 9

Act 5 — Revision Summary

So the bad guy gets it in the end — surprise, surprise... The other big surprise is another load of questions to test whether you <u>really</u> know what happens in Act 5. If you just have a vague, woolly idea of what happens you simply won't be able to write the kind of essay that gets a decent grade. You know the rules — answer all the questions with as much help from Act 5 as you like, and then keep answering them till you don't have to look anything up at all.

1) In <u>Act 5, Scene 1</u>, why has the Gentlewoman called in the Doctor?

2) Write down everything Lady Macbeth does in this scene, in your own words.

3) What is Lady Macbeth gibbering on about when she says "Out, damned spot!"?

4) In lines 53-55, who does Lady Macbeth imagine she is talking to?

5) In <u>Act 5, Scene 2</u>, Angus says "Near Birnam wood/ Shall we meet them" — who is he going to meet?

6) Does Lenox say the soldiers in Siward's army are:
   a) young hooligans, b) young, inexperienced soldiers, c) fierce mercenaries?

7) Write down the exact words used to say each of these things in Act 5, Scene 2.
   a) Macbeth's mad, b) Macbeth's doing up his castle, c) Macbeth's in a rage,
   d) nobody is genuinely loyal to Macbeth, e) he doesn't deserve to be king.

8) In <u>Act 5, Scene 3</u>, Macbeth mentions two of the warnings the apparitions gave him in Act 4, Scene 1. Which one <u>doesn't</u> he mention?

9) What news does the servant bring to Macbeth?

10) Write down a five word quote from lines 20-30 that shows how Macbeth feels.

11) In lines 41-46, Macbeth asks the Doctor if he can cure Lady Macbeth of her troubles. Who else could he be talking about?

12) Which of these best describes Macbeth's attitude to the battle?
    a) he's in a raging hurry to fling himself into it, b) he can take it or leave it.

13) In <u>Act 5, Scene 4</u>, what is the cunning trick Malcolm comes up with to confuse Macbeth's army?

14) In lines 13-14, Malcolm says "none serve with him but constrainèd things/ Whose hearts are absent too." Write this out again in your own words.

15) In <u>Act 5, Scene 5</u>, Macbeth gives his plan for the battle in lines 1-4. What is it?

16) Write down all the descriptions of fear in lines 9-13. Write down the exact words.

17) Who dies during this scene?

18) Write down all the different phrases Macbeth uses to describe life, in lines 17-28.

19) When Macbeth gets the news about Birnam Wood coming to Dunsinane, he changes his plan for the battle. What's he going to do now?

20) Not much happens in <u>Act 5, Scene 6</u>. Sum the scene up in three sentences or fewer.

21) In <u>Act 5, Scene 7</u>, line 1, Macbeth says "they have tied me to a stake". He's not really tied up. What does he mean?

22) Which prediction from Act 4, Scene 1, does Macbeth mention, just after he's killed Young Siward?

23) Who comes on stage, just as Macbeth goes off?

24) Who does Siward say has joined his army, in line 25?

25) In <u>Act 5, Scene 8</u>, what reason does Macbeth give for not fighting Macduff, in lines 5-6?

26) Why is Macduff's speech from lines 13-16 bad news for Macbeth?

27) Macbeth says he'll fight Macduff to the death. What reason does he give, in lines 27-29?

28) In <u>Act 5, Scene 9</u>, what does Macduff carry onto the stage.

29) Who's king now?

30) Write down all the names you can find, used to describe Macbeth, in Act 5.